T0265592

the
unsettled

the
unsettled

small stories of colonisation

RICHARD SHAW

MASSEY UNIVERSITY PRESS

Should I try and pin it down or avoid
it on account of what might lie there?

   – Diana Bridge, 'Deep Colour'

Decolonisation | is your job | not mine

   – Debbie Broughton, 'The re-Taranaki-
   fication of Te Aro Pā'

This book is for Ella Kahu and Trudie Cain, with whom I have exchanged many stories over the years. Some of them have been unsettling in a 'Yup, I definitely needed to be told that' kind of way; many have been about colonisation; each one has been a joy to listen to.

Contents

Prologue

Footy on
the Coast

T HERE IS A PHOTO, A LITTLE DUSTY NOW,
sitting on a shelf in my mother's house. It competes
for space with the novels of Damon Runyon and Niall
Williams, my father's favourite authors. Dad is dead now, gone
these past 10 years. There are photos of him on the shelf, too.

But the one that was at the start of it all is of another man
from another time. He is standing with a group of stern-
looking, formidable men, gazing out across the years. In the
centre, taller than the others, he is holding a ball. The man on
his right has a bandaged head. They are all wearing big, heavy
boots, laces wrapped tightly around their ankles. Behind them
you can just see the hindquarters of a horse.

The photo was taken in 1881 at the Rāhotu Domain, just a
few kilometres away from Parihaka pā. The men are members
of the Armed Constabulary Coastal rugby team. The big man's
name was Andrew Gilhooly. He was the captain of the team,
and my great-grandfather.

I walked past that photo many times over the decades,
looking at it without seeing it. Then Dad died, wheels fell off
here and there, and things that I had not really seen before
began to slide into focus. That photo was one of them. It is a

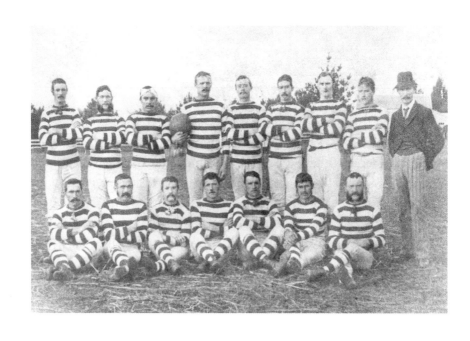

This is just a photo of some blokes ready to play footy, until you put the date (1881), the location (Rāhotu Domain) and the name of the group (the AC rugby team) together. Then it becomes something else entirely. *Richard Shaw*

small thing, this image, but it sits in the context of some very big things. The year, the place, the people — they hint at what is to come. But it took me until my mid-fifties to even start asking the right questions of the photo. What does it have to say about my past? How did I manage, for so long, to miss the story it so obviously tells? What does this all mean for me today? That last one, in particular, is giving me no end of trouble.

And as it turns out, I am not the only person in this country asking it. The circumstances that give rise to the query differ from person to person, as do the responses, but the question itself does not. Neither does it go away if you try to avoid it. It is always there. Waiting.

1.
Find the Beginning

'FIND THE BEGINNING', ADVISES EMILY WILSON, in her beautiful translation of Homer's *Odyssey*.[1] Good advice this, but I find it hard to follow, for there are many possible beginnings to this book. I might have gone with the mid-seventeenth century, when Oliver Cromwell's marauding New Model Army confiscated land in the small Irish township of Ballynagreanagh in the east of County Limerick, beginning a process of impoverishment which will lead my great-grandfather, Andrew Gilhooly, to leave the village of his birth and set sail on his own odyssey 200 years later.[2]

Or I could have chosen 1843, the year in which Andrew's father, Hugh, marries Mary Kennedy, whose family had been ushered onto the farm Andrew was born on by the muscle of the Irish Constabulary following the eviction of the previous tenant for non-payment of rent to an absentee English landlord.[3] Or 1877, the year Andrew signed up for the first of what would be 13 years of military service, the first nine spent in the New Zealand Armed Constabulary (AC) and the balance out in the wind and cold at Port Chalmers, in Otago, where he was a bombardier in the artillery corps of New Zealand's first permanent militia.

Instead, I have chosen 5 November 1881, the day on which my great-grandfather, a member of the AC's No. 3 Company, marched into Parihaka with 1588 other men and tore the place down. He was there for the invasion of the pā established in 1866 by Te Whiti o Rongomai and Tohu Kākahi to provide refuge to those who had suffered other invasions; he was there for the destruction of people's homes and the ruination of their crops; he was there for the years of occupation, during which pass laws were enforced and the hunger bit.[4] He was there, too, for the return, coming back to the Coast in the early 1890s to farm land that was part of the 'great knuckle' of Taranaki and that had been confiscated from mana whenua in 1865.[5]

The three farms Andrew Gilhooly and his wife, Kate Fleming, eventually ran enabled them to break with centuries of Irish penury and reinvent themselves as settlers, members of a tightly knit coastal Taranaki community that orbited around the Catholic church and the family farm. Dispossessed in their own land, they came to Aotearoa and turned themselves into New Zealanders. But they became these new things on land that the colonial state had taken from other people. What was a beginning for them was an ending for others.

None of this was part of the family lore I grew up with (although I did know many other stories about life on the Coast, including the drudgery of milking, the tedium of the Latin mass, and the fortunes of the Taranaki Ranfurly Shield-winning team of the 1950s, which my grandfather Hugh managed).[6] All of it had long since tumbled out of my people's collective memory and fallen down into the dark, forgotten places all families have, replaced on the shelf by our version of the settler story, the one that tells of leaving the old world for the new; that land for this; poverty for something better.[7]

Here are some other things I did not know, once upon a time. For a start, although I had a hazy sense that land had been confiscated from iwi in Taranaki in the mid-1860s, until I reached my fifties I had no idea just how much was taken — some 1,275,000 acres.[8] Neither was I aware that it had been indiscriminately confiscated from 'rebel' and 'loyal' Māori alike (which may explain why, in each of the eight settlements it has negotiated in Taranaki, the Crown has acknowledged that 'the confiscations were indiscriminate in extent and application, wrongful and unjust, and were in breach of the Treaty of Waitangi and its principles'). Ngāti Tama, for instance, lost 74,000 acres. In 1863 the Compensation Court returned 3458 of those acres (just 4.6 per cent of what had been taken) to a number of Ngāti Tama individuals; by 1880 legal title had still not been issued to this land, much of which had, in any event, been reclassified as Crown land in the intervening years.[9]

Neither did I know that the South Road that runs around the Taranaki coast (you'll know it better as State Highway 45, or — if you must — as Surf Highway) was a military road built for the purposes of delivering an invasion force to Parihaka and opening up the land for settlement by Pākehā farmers. My great-grandfather was involved with that, too. The road was the last leg in an invasion infrastructure trifecta, along with the construction of the Cape Egmont lighthouse and the installation of the telegraph.[10]

I had no idea that the suppression of the press meant that it would take two years for full details of what took place at, and after, the invasion of Parihaka — including the forced relocation of over 1,500 people, the rape of women and the destruction of hundreds of acres of crops — to emerge in this country, or that it came to light only because of the insistence of the parliamentary opposition in London that papers to that effect be tabled in the House of Commons.[11]

It had not occurred to me that Parihaka is not just an 'invasion day story'.[12] The AC maintained an occupation force at the pā for nearly five years after the invasion; Major Forster Goring's No. 3 Company — in which my great-grandfather served — finally upped sticks in March 1885. Pass laws restricting the movement of Māori into, out of and within Parihaka first imposed in 1881 were enforced for the duration of the occupation.

I had not heard of the 1882 Indemnity Act, which noted that although 'certain measures adopted by the Government of New Zealand' in the invasion and sacking of Parihaka 'may have been in excess of legal powers', it was found to be 'expedient that the persons acting therein should be indemnified', such that said persons (including my great-grandfather) 'shall be and [are] hereby freed, acquitted, released, indemnified, and discharged of, from, and against all actions, suits, complaints, information, indictments, prosecutions, liabilities, and proceedings whatsoever'.

I did not realise that in 1882, when the Crown finally did get around to giving back some of the land it had taken two decades earlier, it did so in the form of native reserves that were administered not by the Māori owners of the land but by a Crown official, the Public Trustee, who was required to act for both the benefit of 'the natives to whom such reserves belong' and for 'the promotion of settlement'. Unsurprisingly, the second of these imperatives took precedence, and by 1892 control was ebbing away from Māori owners as their land was parcelled out to Pākehā farmers — including my great-grandparents — in leases granted in perpetuity. And for which Māori were ineligible to apply.

Nor did I know that many Māori landowners were charged an occupation licence to live on their own whenua, allowing the Public Trustee 'to decide where on their land they could live and what rent they would have to pay for it'.[13] The licence fee often exceeded the rents Pākehā farmers were charged to farm Māori land, such that people who owned land they could not live on sometimes found themselves in debt. In a letter written in 1909, the Public Trustee helpfully explains that the system was established to 'encourage natives to abandon the communism of their kaingas and to encourage individual effort'.[14]

And I had no earthly notion that sitting behind the title to the farm purchased in 1921 by my great-grandmother, Kate Gilhooly, was an earlier title granted by the Māori Land Court to mana whenua in 1883.[15] The first two names on that title were those of Te Whiti o Rongomai and Tohu Kākahi.[16]

This seems like quite a lot of important stuff not to have known. I stumbled across these things in the process of researching and writing a book, *The Forgotten Coast*, which began as an effort to understand my relationship with my father but wound up as something much bigger.[17] Now that I know them, I find that they cannot be unknown. Neither can I avoid the question they pose — How is it that this detail did not feature in the family lore? — or the conundrum they present — What do I do with the knowledge that my mother's family established itself in this country on land the colonial state had taken from others?

The Forgotten Coast developed into an attempt to get my head around these troubling facets of my family history. It became a vehicle for ending my forgetting. The book included stories about others: my formidable great-grandmother Kate; a great-uncle, Dick, who nailed three degrees at the Pontifical Lateran University in Rome in under two years and then came home to die of TB; and my father, Bob. But it was the stuff about Andrew, the invasion and the three Gilhooly farms that really got people going.

It kicked off late on Friday 16 July 2021, when the online journal *The Conversation* ran a short article I wrote about some of the discoveries at the heart of *The Forgotten Coast*.[18] The experience of writing for *The Conversation* generally goes like this: other media outlets will pick your piece up; reader numbers will spike over a 24-hour period (or sometimes not get off the ground at all); there might be a quick exchange of views via a comments page; and then interest rapidly dies away. This time things were different.

Within minutes the number of people who had read the article started ticking over — and then kept on climbing, so that by the end of the weekend it had received over 100,000 views. Then two unusual things occurred: the readership figures continued to mount and I began receiving a lot of email traffic. After a week the former sat close to 170,000 and the latter was well over 100 (containing, in total, close to 20,000 words, which is about the size of an Honours research paper).[19]

The metrics are not the point. The real significance lies in the content and tone of those emails. Some were short and others lengthy; a number were furious and a handful deeply offensive; a few were disparaging but most were reflective and humbling to read. None of them was humdrum.

It won't surprise anyone that some people were not much taken with what I had to say. I had simply tried to put into words the unease I felt about my great-grandfather's role in the colonial treatment meted out to Taranaki Māori, but what I thought was an attempt at making sense of my own circumstances others saw as something entirely different. Some readers objected to 'academics like you . . . whipping the country with the same old tired guilty stick that all woke people are wielding at the moment', took issue with 'being made to feel like a second class citizen in my own country', and would appreciate it if I 'stop[ped] beating up on the white man for a change'.

Those are some of the more considered contributions. More common were pithy observations such as: 'You are despicable', 'Worst article I have ever read in my life' and 'Appalling drivel and incredibly racist to boot.' The prize for Best in Class for this category, however, goes to the admirably succinct: 'I fell asleep.'

Two of these messages stand out. Both contain spelling errors and other oddities that the pedant in me is tempted to correct — but I've opted not to, because the mistakes tell you something about care, attention and intent, and if I correct them that stuff gets lost. The first of these communications informs me that 'You and the lot you represent in that article aren't welcome in New Zealand any more — and yes, it IS New Zealand. Not Aoteroa. I really fear for impressionable youngsters if you're putting out that dribble. Get a life, little imp.' I'm not sure who I represent but I can categorically say that 'imp' is not something I am often called.

The person who wrote the second didn't bother with arcane language and went straight for the profanity playbook in characterising me as 'just a useless DICK filling young peoples heads with garbage to look good to your fellow racists i bet you cant even change a car tyre DICK, snowflakes like you are a curse on this country . . . who really is only qualified to work at kfc.' This one also came with pictures.

W. B. Yeats's poem 'The Second Coming' is a thing of beauty, all slouchy beasts and collapsing centres. There is a line I think of when I stand back and try to understand the correspondence I received in July 2021. When the dread beast is lumbering towards Jerusalem, Yeats writes, 'The best lack all conviction, while the worst | Are full of passionate intensity.' In my less generous moments I feel as if some of the messages I got were consistent with the second of those observations.

But I part company with Yeats on the convictions of the best, because I also heard from plenty of Pākehā whose stories are not dissimilar to my own: people who have long wondered about the history lying beneath the land they grew up on, and whose disposition towards the ongoing legacy of the colonisation of this country is quite different from that countenanced by proponents of the 'imp' school of thought.

Many of these messages are punchy: a favourite is the suggestion that 'Pākehā feeling exhausted by debate around historic injustice might consider how those who are still living with that injustice might feel'. Quite a few are funny. Two women get in touch, one an Anglican whose 'first marriage was to a Roman Catholic, although (obviously) he was somewhat lapsed', and the other who tells me that her farming grandfather 'always said the kids were brought in with the cows'.

Someone wrote about 'the Irish Catholics on Mum's side and the dodgy land deals on Dad's'. I heard from an elderly man who thought there might very well be something in what I had to say but who I suspect really wanted to tell me that as a youngster he had 'won many athletic medals', even though 'Dad was the one who set all the race records'. And from someone who 'grew up on confiscated land in Hamilton, oblivious to the fact that "Grey Street" was not a reference to a colour'.

Sometimes the humour feels a bit uneasy, as when I hear about 'an old Kaponga identity, a dairy farmer, who told me that when he was young they were sometimes told they should look for a nice Māori wife as this would safeguard their leases for them'. Or about the great-great-grandfather who 'was a bit of a bloodthirsty old codger and no one really liked him, although interestingly enough his father was a prison guard in Tasmania who fought his colleagues to stop the hunting of Indigenous Australians'. Or about the time George Grey visited Arowhenua in Te Wai Pounamu South Island in 1867 to discuss land issues with mana whenua and the welcoming band played Handel's chorus 'See, the Conquering Hero Comes'.[20]

Wry but affectionate judgement is sometimes passed: there is a reference to forebears arriving in Aotearoa with 'their Rule Britannia sensibilities', and another to a 'mysterious great-grandfather (a practised liar) who migrated from Scotland in the 1870s as a farm hand and somehow ended up as a landowner'.

There is poignancy: 'In 1860, an Irish soldier in the 65th Regiment married a young girl, an Irish (?) "settler", in the Catholic chapel erected in New Plymouth for the soldiers. Nine months later she died in childbirth and he disappeared from the historical record. The child survived and became my great-grandmother.' There is insight: 'I'm drawn to the fact that due to my ancestor's actions I am lucky enough to know my family history, whilst the other result of his actions is that I have many Māori friends who don't know their family history as they were lost or displaced.' And there is reflection: 'We speak of how "lucky we are" to have this family land without acknowledging an ignorance of or the forgetting to look for the story behind the one we have conveniently told ourselves.'

Through it all runs an intimate honesty. The work of a brother, a GP, is characterised as 'mopping up the misery of 180 years of colonisation'. A woman speaks of her 'paternal grandfather [who] was a strike-breaker in the 1951 waterside dispute', and about whom she carries regret and sorrow. There is a bloke whose wife's family were 'sent on to Ōpōtiki after Völkner's murder to be part of "pacifying" the district. For pacify read invade. Flourishing farmlands, crops, possessions, villages looted and land confiscated. [He] is given his promised 50 acres but drowns a few months later, leaving [her] and seven kids. But [she] survives, and has 79 grandchildren, including quite a few Māori grandchildren.'

Above all, there is a gentle, insistent questioning. People want to get their heads around the knotty stuff. Want to end their own forgetting. Many of them ask: 'What should we do now?'

It strikes me, then, that the best do not lack conviction at all. There are other Pākehā like me out there who have no wish to maintain a personal silence on the matter of our colonial history and would much prefer to get stuck into making sense of things we find complex and troubling. Who have chosen not to cleave only to those bits of our families' (and nation's)

histories that reflect well on us, and who understand that we need also to find ways of living with those episodes that bring discomfort and unease. No 'slipping through the back door of the world' for this lot.[21]

I've heard from former police inspectors and lay preachers (and from one person who has been both); from a group of middle-aged friends who meet online fortnightly to 'collectively work through books (*White Fragility, Me and White Supremacy*), and share thought-provoking articles, podcasts, films, interviews, etc., as we come across them'; and from two sisters who were part of the campaign to change the name of a small town in south Taranaki from Maxwell to Pākaraka.[22] (And with good reason. On 27 November 1868 the Kai Iwi Cavalry — a local militia group led by the future native minister John Bryce — ran into a group of children of Ngaa Rauru Kiitahi and other Taranaki iwi at Handley's Woolshed, near Waitōtara. The cavalry fired at the children, the oldest of whom was 10, then attacked them with sabres. Two children were killed and others wounded. Until recently the town was named after the cavalry's sergeant, George Maxwell.)[23]

People have got in touch from rural New Zealand and urban Aotearoa. They have been curt, wise, forthcoming, sometimes cagey and, yes, occasionally abusive. I've heard from artists and activists, current nuns and former priests, chairs of boards of trustees, farmers, librarians, Māori, men with degrees and women who left school without anything, men who left school with nothing and women with PhDs, middle managers, mums and dads (together and apart), parents, grandparents and great-grandparents, people with partners and those who live alone, some who call themselves Pākehā and others who prefer European (but no one who opts for Kiwi), twins, teachers, teenagers, trampers, working people and retired people, widows and widowers, young people and old, the lot. I've also exchanged views with at least one novelist, a Danish seaman, an award-winning scientist, a bus driver, a hunter, a mechanic, a psychotherapist and a mother/daughter combo — and with someone who badly wants to renounce his New Zealand citizenship but isn't being allowed to do so (for reasons I simply could not follow, but which he assures me are available for all to see on his 'Webb-site').

I have come to this party late, but many of these folk are well on their way. We do not always agree with each other. But whether or not we are in accord, the message I have received from this vast and varied correspondence is that there are many people in Aotearoa New Zealand who reject the lazy tropes about the civilising effects of colonisation, and who want instead to be part of a more honest conversation about the past from which we have emerged and the future we might yet reach.

This book is a contribution to that discussion.

'You'll write your one story many ways,' says a writing teacher in Elizabeth Strout's novel *My Name Is Lucy Barton*.[24] What she means, I think, is that each of us has only one biography but as time passes we tell that story in different ways. *The Unsettled* is not a sequel to *The Forgotten Coast*. It is less biographical, for a start, and its roots lie not in one place but in many. Dick remains on the Coast, as does my father.

But Andrew, who was at the centre of that earlier book, has made the leap across into this one. The conundrums created by his participation in the invasion of Parihaka and subsequent farming of confiscated land — and those which confront the other people you will encounter here — are what propel this narrative.

Nor is this book a history of colonisation (although it contains quite a few stories about it), a scholarly exposé or an attempt to offer advice. Its purpose is to reflect on some gnarly questions that people in this country are increasingly asking themselves. Why have parts of some Pākehā people's pasts been forgotten? What happens if those forgotten accounts, when dragged from the depths of memory, reveal family histories that are entangled in the violence of the colonisation of this place? How do descendants of settler-colonial families deal with these kinds of backstories? What do we do with that awareness, and how do we talk about it? So many questions that could so comfortably remain rhetorical, but that the people whose accounts inform this book have directly confronted.

To end the forgetting, of course, you must find a beginning. *The Unsettled* is also about the process of recovering these lost elements, what that experience can lead to and what might then be done with often unsettling discoveries. It is really a book about excavation.

Those doing the digging are ordinary people. Probably not all that different from the ones you work with, live next door to or go to church with; the sort you might bump into at the dairy or chew the fat with while waiting for the kids to come barrelling out of school. Probably quite a bit like the ones you love and share your life with.

You will hear their voices alongside mine as we wander 'up and down the hills and dales' of what is a challenging conversation.[25] Some nip in for a quick word, then disappear; others linger and get stuck into a sustained discussion. A number have asked not to be named, but some want to stand in public alongside their words. Aidan, for instance, who is 21, works in the agribusiness/rural banking sector in Ōtepoti Dunedin and has family in Taranaki. Dorothy and David, she once a teacher and he a civil engineer, are now both up to their necks in local and family histories. Gillian is of Clan MacBain, Clan Cameron, Clan Lyon and Clan Grant, and is a writer of many forms (among them a student newspaper, a feminist magazine and novels). Jane was brought up on a farm leased from Māori at Puniho, just south of Ōkato, as was her younger brother Tim, although both have long since moved away (Tim taking with him the memory of once 'having pāua and porridge for breakfast' at a mate's place, which wasn't standard fare at home).

Joe was with the New Zealand Police for over 30 years, the last 16 as an inspector, and resigned to become a lay pastoral leader after walking the Camino de Santiago. John, who lives in Kaipara, has tramped all of Tītokowaru's battle sites, and has a good friend who is a descendant of Robert Parris, the civil commissioner in Taranaki whom we meet a little further on, for he has a part to play in the construction of the road down which my great-grandfather and his AC comrades walked into infamy in 1881.

Justine, who is 'of both Pākehā and Māori descent, but raised within a Pākehā context', moved around a lot as a child and now manages a team involved in environmental projects in Māngere; her mum, Win, who lives in Kapanga Coromandel, spent a working life attending to people's various medical, spiritual or dental requirements. Kiaran, who hails from Levin but grew up on a farm in Kaponga, has spent most of his life in the motor trade (including driving mini-buses around Europe in the summer of 1969). Marguerite was raised in Kaiapoi and, following a stint in corporate America (and a PhD), has lived in Sydney, but her roots on this side of the Ditch reach back to her grandmother, who crocheted altar cloths for St Peter's Anglican Church in Temuka.

Susan once lived in Montreal amongst Estonians, Latvians, Lithuanians, French, Czechs, Hungarians, Austrians and Greeks but is now, at 81, retired in West Auckland. Another Susan, who I will call Susan Elizabeth, is a nun with the Congregation of Our Lady of the Missions: she, too, has a doctorate, and is in the throes of completing a history of her order in Burma.

I would like to explain why I have used the word 'unsettled' in the title of this book. As far as I can tell, David, Gillian, Jane and the rest are all perfectly well-adjusted people: they are settled, in the conventional sense of the word. But two things are going on in this story, and for them, that are decidedly unsettling.

The first is that they are disturbed by aspects of their families' histories in Aotearoa. I suspect many of us are, if we allow ourselves to stop and think about it. There are fragments of our pasts — Win's 'unsaid, difficult things' — that we glimpse out of the corners of our eyes but do not fully apprehend; things that are hinted at and which make us uneasy, and that jar with the vigorous, uncomplicatedly positive pioneer stories we Pākehā grow up with.

We grapple with these in ways which differ in their particulars and intensity but which are similar in intent. Confronting our family's past — asking questions of the narratives through which our people explain themselves to each other — is an unavoidably unsettling thing to do, and liable to get us into trouble if we do not tread carefully.

For it is the job of these intimate family stories to put shape around a particular group of people, to create a sense of how and where they fit in the world. American literary scholar Jonathan Gottschall would say that we are creatures of stories, which is another way of saying that these things really do matter.[26] People are invested in their family stories, and with good reason, and so it is no small nor easy thing to start prodding them. Sometimes it is dangerous, and nearly always it is disturbing. To have things that did not feature in the accounts we grew up with slouch into view can be unnerving — the more so when they concern matters that go to the heart of the colonial past and present of the country we live in.

This suggests the second sense in which the term 'unsettled' describes what happens in these pages. And that is that my collaborators are also conscious of the *un*settling effects the arrival of their settler families in this land have had on those who were here before.

Not all of them have histories that are as directly implicated in colonial violence as mine is. Nevertheless, the thread connecting us all is an awareness that in some way each of our lives is what it is because at some point someone, somewhere, benefited from colonisation. As Gillian puts it: 'This is how we've become who we are now.' For some, that legacy is decidedly uncomfortable.

We are figuring out, too, that the consequences of injustices perpetrated in the past tend to endure and accumulate. Land has not been returned, taonga are still lost, futures remain forgone. Consigning these losses to times long gone is simply a way of avoiding acknowledging that many things that were done then continue to have ramifications now. It amounts to choosing not to see the thread that ties, for good or ill, our own presents to others' pasts. Some of us get to make this choice — others have to endure its consequences. Daily.

But this isn't what the people who appear in this book are doing: they're taking a different, harder path. They're building up the stamina needed to see through the historical whitewashing and to have the challenging conversations that lie ahead.[27] They're trying to figure out how to live well, not just with those around them but also with their own pasts, presents and possible futures. They may be unsettled, but if so they are doing something about it.

They send me things, those who I have come to think of affectionately as 'my people' or simply as 'us'. Scribbled notes, beautifully researched and self-published family histories, poetry, PowerPoint presentations prepared for sceptical Pākehā colleagues, a letter and a Christmas card written by Princess Te Puea Hērangi, old images of Parihaka I have never seen before.[28] There's a history of the Sisters of Our Lady of the Mission (about which I know a bit, as one of my aunties was a member of that order), beautiful prose concerning time spent in a kitchen on a marae, images of stamps, maps. Lots of other stuff — the intimate paraphernalia of lives lived.

With several I develop an enriching correspondence. Mary speaks of a compassionate Catholicism without priests; Susan Elizabeth (who knows Mary well) tells me stories from the frontline of a religious order (and they are not the sorts of things I recall the nuns of my childhood saying). Gillian writes of what it means to be a descendant of John Bryce, the native

This image of Parihaka, by Australian artists Frank Mahony and A. H. Fullwood, was completed in the 1880s. Tohu Kākahi and Te Whiti o Rongomai have returned, resistance has resumed and Parihaka is building back from the destruction wrought by the invasion and occupation. *National Library of Australia,* Picturesque Atlas of Australasia, *1886–89, PA 575. Thanks to Gary Wersky, from the Department of History, University of Sydney*

minister who worked tirelessly to manufacture the invasion of Parihaka and who, on 5 November 1881, rode into the pā on his white charger.

Marguerite tells of the sense of responsibility that comes with being a descendant of people who farmed on land that once belonged to Ngāi Tahu. Dorothy talks about the slow, methodical work she and David have embarked on, at the end of which they will have digitised the entire Record Book of the New Zealand AC. John sends me a history he has written of his wife's people, which I devour in one sitting. Then read again.

Many speak of the discussions they have and continue to have with family members. None of them confuse these conversations with 'the truth': they are all, as far as I can tell, entirely aware of former academic Keith Ovenden's reminder that 'a lot of what we profess to know is derived from what others tell us' (and therefore subject to all of the caveats associated with the veracity and scope of other people's powers of recall).[29]

Some can buttress family recollections with artefacts from the formal archival record, but for those from humble beginnings and whose families left no enduring visible stamp on history, the oral tradition is all there is. For each of them, however, it is the why as well as the what of their families' origins in this place that engages, and a 'faithfulness to uncertainty' that sustains.[30] Living with discomfort is pretty much a prerequisite for the excavators. Closure, not so much.

And they talk. At one presentation I gave on *The Forgotten Coast* a former minister of the Crown stood and fulminated — at length and with considerable emotion — against the constitutional outrages (his words, not mine) perpetrated by the colonial administration prior to and following the invasion of Parihaka. He was referring to episodes such as Native Minister Bryce's cavalier attitude to constitutional fundamentals in the parliamentary debate concerning the Confiscated Land Inquiry and Maori Prisoners' Trials Act 1879, which gave the governor of the colony the right to defer the trials of the 420 Parihaka ploughers arrested in May 1879 and imprisoned without charge in Hokitika, Dunedin and on Rīpapa Island in Lyttelton Harbour.[31] Warned that 'by passing this measure the House would be indorsing a species of legislation of a very dangerous and unprecedented character', Bryce airily dismissed both Magna Carta and the principle of *habeas corpus* as 'mere legal technicalities', suggesting that the latter 'might become a curse for a country if it could not be set aside when occasion demanded it'.[32] The ex-politician who rose to speak at my presentation was deeply affronted by his predecessor's proto-populist demonstration of casual constitutional expediency.

Here is another account of the distress that can attach to your past. Following a talk at the Palmerston North Probus Club, an elderly Pākehā woman approaches and asks quietly if we might talk. We can, and do, and her account is a moving one. She had grown up on a farm in the Waitōtara Valley in south Taranaki. There was an urupā on the farm, around which stood a series of carved pou. She remembers that before her father sold the farm in the 1940s he, having heard on the Pākehā grapevine that the new owner intended to cut them down, removed each of the pou and presented them to the local museum — which promptly sold them to an overseas collector.[33] It is this that brings her to tears as we talk, this intense distress she still carries, 80 or so years later, that the pou remain far from home.

At a gathering at the Ōkato Coastal School I refer to another urupā, this one on the land my great-grandmother purchased in 1921. My mother and her cousin, both of whom spent time on that farm as kids, recall this urupā — they remember that it was fenced off from the cows and they were not allowed near it. I have visited the farm in recent years and the current owner is not sure that it still exists. But after the talk a kuia comes up and tells me that it very much does exist — and she would know, because her husband is buried there.

I give a presentation in Tāhuna Queenstown, at which a Pākehā man bemoans that all of the attention being given to Māori these days means that he is being made to feel like a second-class citizen in his own land. There are hisses from some in the audience. Tears, too, from a woman in row three who is deeply distressed that racism is the only explanation she has to hand for the treatment meted out to Māori by the poor of Ireland and Scotland who did the dirty work of colonisation. She wishes for better from her people, who were themselves the victims of British colonisation in their own homelands.

None of what 'my people' have to say — whether in person, prose or poetry — is self-serving. Much of it is remarkable. All of it is humbling — and it unsettles them.

One more thing. The voices of tangata whenua are seldom in the spotlight in this book. Writer and historian Rachel Buchanan (Taranaki, Te Ātiawa) has taught me many things, one of which is that there are some stories which are not mine to tell. I have tried to take that lesson to heart — as I have the reciprocal obligation to tell the ones that *are* mine to tell, and to engage in the conversations we Pākehā need to be having amongst ourselves. Conversations are simply exchanges of stories, and the tales I want to hear are of and about Pākehā. As Marguerite puts it, you might not be able to undo your history but you can acknowledge wrong where it has been done — and that needs Pākehā to tell their stories and to talk about their histories.

Some will take issue with this, and see in it the sidelining of Māori. But Pākehā are placed centre stage here so that a bright light can be shone on matters which are otherwise too easily avoided. Too often we look to Māori to make us feel better about ourselves ('Tell us your history and teach us your language, and then tell us what good people we are for having taken an interest in both'), and I do not wish to do that by scuttling off into the wings and watching the action from side-stage. Tangata whenua are on every single page of this book: they stand behind all the broken contracts, each acre of confiscated land and every attempt to demean, diminish or disparage Māori.[34]

But the conversations I would like to have are with those who have been part of the long process by which colonisation has turned Aotearoa into New Zealand, regardless of which oceans their people crossed to get here or when they voyaged — because we all share a common 'political ancestry' (if not a genealogical one) that reaches back to colonisation.[35] We are the ones who need to get our stories straight. Tangata whenua have enough to be getting on with. This is our work.

A last word on this. I don't disagree with University of Auckland professor Alex Calder, who weighs in against 'the invention of incommensurable differences between Maori and

Pakeha' and prefers 'the give and take of the ever-changing beach, where warring incompatibilities dissolve in the middle ground'.[36] Former Anglican bishop John Bluck, too, rightly points to the histories, lives and stories in which Māori and Pākehā are intertwined.[37] But while I share Calder's distaste of binaries and Bluck's embrace of that which is shared, in this book I am not looking for the points of intersection and overlap. I want the gaze to be fairly and squarely on how the incompatibilities came to exist (and to endure) in the first place. I think that has to happen before anything can dissolve.

2.

Small
Stories

ALL FAMILIES HAVE ORIGIN MYTHS. NOT THE big nation-building narratives forged in the great theatres of parliaments, government departments or court rooms, but the small stories gathering together and binding the everyday acts and events that take place in homes and houses; at births, weddings and funerals; and in churches, committee meetings and clubrooms.[1]

These small stories are how we make sense of where we have come from; they are one of the ways in which families communicate their memories.[2] Beyond those to whom they belong, they are generally thought to be not all that important in the grand historical sweep of things, rarely finding their way into museums, exhibitions or other holders of historical record. But they are, for they do all sorts of important work.

In settler-colonial societies like ours, one of their jobs is to stake a claim to being here. For many Pākehā, the emotional labour of asserting our place in and on this land falls to our chronicles of long sea journeys, hardship and privation; to our tales of how the land was broken in and years of struggle endured while families were formed and new lives built.

These sorts of stories are also our first and most enduring histories, learned not in classrooms but in the places where we gather to remember and recount what has gone before. We dust them off and give them a run at family gatherings. Some are lengthy sagas and others you whip through in no time. There are no set texts for these histories: they are part of an oral tradition, soaked up by listening to the keepers of the memories and tellers of the tales. They shape how we see our past, create a shared meaning for those who live in the present and carry a version of ourselves into the future. But they also hide things. In all families there are experiences that are not spoken of. For these reasons, too — for their gaps and absences — our small stories need to be taken seriously.

None of the origin stories I've been told is like another, but each shares threads with the rest. They nearly always start with a moment in time when history begins: the genesis back to which all that has since come to pass is traced. The year the boat sailed from the old country, say, or in which it arrived in the new land; the purchase of the family farm and the start of the hard work of pioneering; the beginning of the family tree.[3] The point in the past beyond which there is no further past.

Now and then the voyage out here is itself a character in the story. Tales of arduous ocean crossings serve not only to underscore the permanence of leaving but also to mark out our forebears as just the sorts of hardy folk a new colony needs. My great-grandfather's trip on the *Wennington* from Gravesend to Wellington in early 1874 took 124 days (rather than the usual 100 or so). Three children died and 10 were born during the four months Andrew was at sea, the *Wellington Independent* noting on the ship's arrival that 'it is, at all events, a great thing to know that after all her long voyage, there is nothing serious, if anything at all, in the shape of disease on board'.

Andrew's future brother-in-law Michael Fleming, who also left from Gravesend in 1874, made it out on the *Michael Angelo* in just 81 days — but the death toll was higher (eight, including the ship's captain) and the number of births lower (just three). And some 20 years later Michael's brother Thomas survived three shipwrecks before finally washing up in New Zealand, the family long since having given him up for dead. No one these days knows the particulars, but those shipwrecks are an important part of our family lore.

Every so often something marks the end of the journey. Joe tells me that the first branch of his family arrived in this country in 1839 and that William Green promptly swam 'some cattle ashore at Green's Point, Akaroa' (where a sewage plant is now located). Another branch of the family was on board the *William Bryan*, the first of the New Zealand (Plymouth) Company ships to dock in New Plymouth when it berthed in 1841. 'The Climo family,' Joe says, 'had land allocated at Tataraimaka, just south of New Plymouth, and one of them was wounded in the battle of Waireka. They were evacuated to Nelson and never got that land back.'[4]

Jane's great-great-great-grandmother Elizabeth and her six children left their 'home in the country' and were also shipped south at the outbreak of the Taranaki wars; her husband, who was in the militia and ran supplies from New Plymouth to the AC at Ōpunake, remained behind. But Elizabeth and the kids returned when the war was finished, and 'the family settled on a 50-acre soldiers' land grant on Koru Road in a house built of timber from the Fort Niger blockhouse in New Plymouth'.

Many of these foundation stories are really tales of escape; of taking flight from old social and economic strictures in other countries that kept people in their place. In Andrew Gilhooly's case, that place was a 29-acre piece of land leased by his father on terms that gave the family no security of tenure. My great-grandfather is described as an Irish labourer in both the *Wennington*'s manifest and the AC's Description Book — a description unlikely to have changed had he stayed in Ireland. Whatever my reservations about what he did when he got here, I can understand why he might have wanted to leave.[5]

Others, too, were impelled to get away: from the English in general, or from the squalor, poverty and disease of the industrial wastelands of the big cities. From the press gangs, religious repression and the suffocation of the class system. From the poorhouse (where one of Gillian's ancestors, 'born two generations after Culloden and now landless, died of bedsores around the time his son sailed here with his own young family') or the workhouse (the Brampton iteration of which had also claimed a few of Gillian's forebears). So many good reasons to leave such terrible things behind.

Many came of their own volition but some did not. In his history of his wife's ancestors, John explains that the path Trudi's great-great-grandparents took began with transportation from Ireland to Tasmania. During the Great Famine, Bridget Lee was sentenced to seven years' transportation for stealing sheep (much later, a history of women's suffrage in Ōpōtiki would claim that she was moved to leave Ireland 'by the spirit of adventure and a desire for a better life'),[6] while her future husband, John Kelly, received the same sentence for taking a sheet and a nightdress.[7] In time they would wind up in Ōpōtiki, but it wouldn't be planned and it began with a long voyage in a convict ship. Heartbreakingly, Bridget is described in the records of Dublin's Grangegorman prison as 'a good girl'.

'Escaping from' also means striking out towards, the former all too familiar, the latter mostly imagined — be it a blurry sense of a better life or something more substantive. John's own predecessors were part of the great wave of migration out of Cornwall in the second part of the nineteenth century.[8] 'They were Primitive Methodists,' he says, 'and I can see in their lives another great theme of New Zealand history: egalitarianism. They were involved in the growth of unionism, the workers' educational associations, suffrage, temperance and community institutions.'

Clarity of purpose was also a characteristic of Gillian's great-grandparents who, on her father's side, 'were early members of the Fabian Society, and William Morris' Socialist League when they lived in London during the 1880s; they also lived in Toynbee Hall, a socialist university settlement in Whitechapel, and later helped finance *The Clarion* newspaper'.[9] After arriving in New Zealand in 1900, William and Margaret Ranstead 'arranged the passage of around 200 socialists and their families here, in the same year, to form a socialist settlement. That never quite happened, though some started the Socialist Party in 1901, or became part of the first Labour government in 1935.'

These were people on a mission. That the vaulting ideal did not quite find material expression for William and Margaret Ranstead is not, perhaps, the point: '[I]f the dream of a socialist world faded somewhat,' Gillian reflects, 'they were still able to create the older image of a clachan, based on kinship bonds and spreading outwards. They lived handsomely, openly, and were known far and wide for their hospitality, kindness and learning; the family friends, Māori and Pākehā, ranged across the social spectrum.'

Sometimes, however, the better life is the one left behind. Gillian's grandmother on her mother's side, her Nana, 'knew the stories of the family's demise after the battle of Culloden, but preferred to go farther back to the days when our ancestors were the kings and queens of ancient Scotland. For her, the past 200 years or so of hardship and poverty were a mere aberration in the thousands of years of our history, and certainly no excuse for behaving or dressing badly.'

Rising to challenges is also a mainstay of the narrative template. The obstacles were sometimes formidable. In the mid-1860s John Kelly left Launceston, Tasmania, to find work in Melbourne. For a time he sent money back to Bridget, but he soon began sending it to the local publican instead. In desperation, Bridget made her way to Melbourne with her children, only to discover that John had disappeared, having signed up with the 1st Waikato Militia in Melbourne and sailed for New Zealand, attracted by the promise of land (50 acres for a private).

She was forced to return to Launceston and was left stranded — 'unprovided for' — with five children. With the help of the Tasmanian authorities she eventually managed to scramble across the Tasman with the little ones, only for John to drown in the Waioeka River a couple of years later — leaving her 'unprovided for' once again.[10] By this time, Bridget had seven children, the youngest just two months old. The portents were not good.

A river claimed John Kelly, and the physical environment also challenged others. Win's maternal grandparents 'came to farm in the inland Gisborne area, then later in inland Taranaki. I grew up hearing stories of their hard work "clearing" the land in remote and rugged country, and of losing a number of children to illness and accident. They were resourceful, practical and hardworking.'

For Jane, an intriguing part of the family story is about the forebears who 'were granted land at Kāwhia on the condition that they spent six months of the year on that land. They drove stock from Taranaki along the coast to Kāwhia. In order to get past White Cliffs at Mount Messenger those men involved created a tunnel just north of the cliffs so they could get through between the tides.' That tunnel is still there and is part of the White Cliffs walkway.

Further south, three Fleming brothers bought land on the Cape Road from the Crown in the early 1880s. Before the cows could be let loose on it, however, the brothers had to clear it of flax. Flax was big business in Taranaki: there were nine mills operating between Ōkato and Oaonui.[11] Harvesting the harakeke was backbreaking work, but the men received five shillings per ton from the Rutherfords, whose mill was at the bottom of the Lower Parihaka Road. Soon enough the land was clear and the dairying could begin in earnest.

Cows in Taranaki; a different kind of business up in Auckland. 'The ancestral line of my family,' someone else writes, 'came to Aotearoa New Zealand on the ship *London* in December 1840.' They were bakers and carpenters from Devon, and were 'most likely exposed to the promises of Edward Gibbon Wakefield to make a new life'. A year after they arrived they 'went on to Tāmaki Makaurau Auckland in 1841 and developed a significant business there which included felling trees, hauling and milling logs, stacking and cutting boards, then employing carpenters and joiners to make doors, windows and whole houses and government buildings'.

My correspondent was unsure whether they 'had involvement in the land wars, or how they procured the timber for their milling business' (nor does she know 'much about the lives of women in the family'), but she is sure that 'at the time they arrived in this country there were only about 2000 Pākehā here, so clearly they needed to develop business and personal relationships with Māori'. If so, that part of the story has not been passed down.

Justine's forebears on her mother Win's side were people from the Isle of Man, Scotland and Ireland who figured out how to farm the land they bought after arriving in this country. They 'were hard working, clearing the land to create farms, growing their own food, generating their own power, building their own houses, and learning how to do all of this "on the job". They were resourceful people and were just doing what they needed to do to make a life here.' Adept at 'winning order from wilderness', Justine's family make today's weekend DIYers look like slackers.[12]

As for her father's people, Justine knew from childhood 'that an ancestor had come from the UK as an orphaned child, after losing his convict parents in Australia. The child was brought up on Mana Island on a sheep farm, but spent a lot of time with local Māori, who taught him their language. He eventually became an interpreter for the Māori land courts and the New Zealand Company.' It occurs to her, these days, that 'the overwhelming narrative was of the hard life he had, rather than the damage the New Zealand Company did to Māori, or his part in it'.

Sometimes the physical environment was not the only adversary. My great-grandmother Kate's two older brothers, Michael and Richard Fleming, were among the first dairy farmers on the Taranaki coast, and provided milk and butter for the AC's Pungarehu contingent (which included Kate's future husband, Andrew). An account of their travails casually notes that '[m]any were the hardships to be endured at this time and it was only their faith, courage and strength of character that enabled those two brothers to carry on. The Maori Wars were not yet ended and many troublesome times were endured.'[13]

In fact, there's a bit more to this story. On 19 October 1881 Lieutenant-Colonel Roberts, the AC's commanding officer in Taranaki, sent a cable to Sir John Hall, the premier, in Wellington, reporting that 'Fleming and his mate were working in the bush on Section 22 this morning, cutting and carrying out posts, when about fifty Maoris came to them and told them to leave off work, at the same time carrying back the posts which Fleming had carried to the road-side.

'At first they spoke only in Maori, but subsequently told them in English to stop. Besides this, over two hundred small posts for a sod-and-wire fence, which were laid along the road frontage of 28, have been carried off the land, and thrown into the flax and fern, and some into a swamp.'[14]

A few other details slip through. As I pore over the archival record I come across oblique references to 'squabbles with the Maoris' and to 'the Te Whiti troubles', but nothing amounts to much because 'the maoris become their very good and firm friends' and narrative order is quickly restored.

Whatever (or whoever) the adversary, perseverance and application nearly always triumphed. It is important that this happened, because breaking with the past is central to the colonial mythos [15] The belief that this is a country where people can transform themselves through hard work is elemental; it is what is said on the colonial tin. And it is often what happened — although sometimes only after a rough start. In or around 1875, someone tells me, 'an Irish Catholic immigrant', an ancestor on the Irish side of the family, 'deserted his four young daughters, son and wife and went to Australia to live, where he died alone in 1899. The mother, who had arrived in New Zealand with her Irish siblings, was charged with prostitution, resulting in her daughters being brought up in a Nelson convent and attending St Mary's Industrial School.'

But the colonial project delivered, and the break with the past duly arrived. My interlocutor's great-grandparents, who owned an accommodation business and a nearby farm, 'had nine children who became well educated and reasonably affluent. The next generation was mostly tertiary educated (mainly lawyers and teachers), and they produced a wide range of professionals, including doctors, ecologists, engineers, lawyers, pilots, economics graduates and so on.'

Success was not, of course, a given. I heard from someone whose ancestors 'left England to escape the dominant class structure', and who acquired 'vast tracts of Wairarapa land by possibly dubious means' which were 'never spoken about'. (By design rather than carelessness, it would appear, my correspondent being '[f]airly sure that the lack of any family recollections of how they came to own the land would be quite deliberate. No conscience and no guilt.') But this person's father 'managed to lose his share of the family inheritance through incompetence and alcoholism'.

From time to time the towel was thrown in and the long haul home undertaken, the realisation having dawned that things were not, in fact, better here than they were there. An advertisement was placed in a Cornish newspaper by a 'steady and industrious engineman' who asked for a collection to be raised to help him return home, his having had 'bad luck' in New Zealand.[16]

There is always a chapter in our small stories on building things up and putting roots down. This bit speaks of families — Gillian's 'magnificent array of aunties, uncles, great-aunties, great-uncles and more cousins than I could count' — and communities, and of the ties that bind people together and keep them tethered to a land that can be unforgiving. The places where this work is done — the tables at which meals are eaten, the clubs where sports are played, the places of worship — help us stick. Then and now.

Sometimes the ties are remarkably resilient. 'In 1906 William and Margaret bought land in Matangi that by then had been bought and sold a few times since being confiscated,' Gillian says, 'though there was, and still is, a strong presence of the mana whenua, Te Rangitaupi of Ngāti Hauā. The farm was later shared amongst their sons, who built homes up and down the same road; their daughters lived a few miles north. There were 20 grandchildren growing up together; in time, there were 60 or so great-grandchildren, some of us living a little farther away, most nearby, but we were all of us part of the one family.' These are people who adhere.

For some, religion is one of the most important of the ties that bind. It is certainly central to my story, largely as a consequence of the wave of 'Irish episcopal imperialism' that

swept across the English-speaking Catholic world, washing
away the French Marists who were the first Catholic foot
soldiers in this country.[17]

The French order, however, had ways of leaving its mark.
Mary Josephine Genevieve Fleming was born out at Cape
Egmont in June 1886: she was baptised by an Irish priest but
her third name was the legacy of an earlier Marist tradition
of adding a French saint's name to the mix. Later, Mary won
a scholarship to attend New Plymouth Girls' High School.
Her mother sent her to the Catholic convent instead, fearful
that the irreligious girls at the public school would endanger
her daughter's spiritual health — no small concern, given that
the consequences would have been eternal.

In my family religion got personal. Dick, Kate and Andrew's
boy, was the A-lister, his triumphs abroad bringing considerable
reflected glory on the Gilhoolys, and on a coastal Catholic
community which claimed him as one of their own. They gave
him a huge shindig when he left for Rome in 1930, some 700 of
them gathering to send him off and to hand over a well-filled
wallet of notes at the end of the night.

There were others, too. My uncle Sam — who once
brought me an Easter egg the size of a football — spent two
years in Dick's old seminary but found his real vocation in
a different institution, the military. Sam's older sister Cath,
the first of the 11 children my grandmother Milly gave birth
to, made a much better fist of religious life. Cath's religious
name was Sister Mary Richard (I think partially in homage
to her uncle), and for 50 years she was a member of the
Congregation of Our Lady of the Missions. She was a gun maths
teacher, deft with a needle, and filled in when her kids' rugby
teams were short. Her favourite biblical passage was from

Micah: 'To live justly, to love tenderly, and to walk humbly with your God.'

Religion gives structure and meaning in others' stories, too, including those of John's Primitive Methodist forebears, who brought with them (and put into impressive effect) an enduring commitment to egalitarianism. Other religious links are more surprising. Jane's grandfather Roy was shot during the First World War in a battle which took the life of his brother Monty. Roy would have been the second son killed that day (and Jane would not have been Jane) had it not been for the Bible he carried in his chest pocket, which took the brunt of incoming fire and saved his life. 'I had that Bible until 1983,' Jane muses, 'when it was stolen.'

Sport, too, was a big deal. Andrew's sons Hugh and Tom would ride their big, heavy bikes ('grids', my dad used to call them when he was a boy) into New Plymouth and back to watch the Friday-night boxing. It was a round trip of 50 kilometres along a winding gravel road that had carried an invasion force long before it delivered Hugh and Tom to the big smoke. A third son, Andy, was a prolific sports administrator, throwing himself into anything involving bikes, boxing, axes or athletics. Dogs, too.

And the rugby — always the rugby, and with good reason, for Hugh was a stalwart of the sport in Taranaki, presiding over the Rāhotu club for two decades and chairing the Taranaki Rugby Football Union between 1949 and 1958.[18] Of the Gilhooly women's sporting involvement there is scant record, although I imagine it often fell to Hugh to thank them for refreshments.

Sport also consumed Jane's great-great-grandfather Frank, although he was an actual athlete rather than an administrator, 'winning many events on the coast between 1884 and 1887

51

and the Caledonian Cup at Hāwera in 1887. He was, moreover, a wrestler and a good bowler in his later years, winning the Taranaki Singles Bowling Championship in 1934 aged 71.' Frank also mastered the piano and was much 'in demand to play the fiddle at Military Balls and other dances'. An allrounder, then.

Seen from the distance of a century or so, the number and range of community organisations into which people poured themselves is breathtaking. Marguerite's grandmother was active in three churches (St Peter's Anglican Church in Temuka, the Arowhenua Pā church and St John's in Winchester), and in organisations including the Red Cross, the local library, the Mechanics' Institute, the Arowhenua Māori Ladies Guild and the Māori Women's Institute. Jane's great-great-grandmother Emma was a founding member of the Ōpunake Women's Division of Federated Farmers; and sundry other members of her family threw themselves into the Ōpunake Mardi Gras, the Taranaki (and New Zealand) Pig Councils and the Pātea Hospital Board — when they weren't driving school buses, playing the piano for silent movies or tending the blooms in a champion Begonia House.

Setting aside various rugby clubs, between them Hugh, my grandfather, and his brother Andy were members of 15 different organisations. Line them up one after another and they invoke the dense social ties that knitted these men with others in their community. Take a deep breath, then, and recite after me: the Pungarehu school committee, the Taranaki Hospital Board, the Rāhotu Athletic Club, the Cape Egmont Dog Trials Club, the Loyal Rāhotu Lodge, the Egmont County Council (and sub-committees), the New Plymouth Cycling and Athletic League, the Coastal Boxing Association, the Rāhotu Hall Committee, the Cape Egmont Dairy Company, Federated

Farmers, the Young Farmers' Club, the Rāhotu Manchester
Unity of the Order of Oddfellows, the St Pius X Catholic Church
Committee, and the Taranaki Centre of the New Zealand
Athletic, Cycling and Axemen's Union.

There is something in these words, the cadence very nearly
coming together into something lyrical. But it doesn't quite
happen. Instead, the list collapses into a litany of times past.
Just a handful of these organisations still exist, the rest long
since shuttered and mothballed, the people having moved
off the land and the years having moved on. Perhaps the ties
frayed, or the roots were too shallow.

Big characters often stand astride our small stories. The
eponymous forebear who was the first to leave there or to arrive
here; the formidable matriarch who kept the family together
during the darkest of hours; the ancestor who did something
extraordinary or who had something extraordinary done to
them. Someone who stands out or looms over a family, and
thereby provides narrative focus to the entire story.

For Marguerite it is her grandmother, Mary Ellen Foxon, who
in addition to crocheting altar cloths for the local church was
involved in the Mechanics' Institute (a forerunner of the Workers
Educational Authority), played ladies' hockey in skirts that were
just above the ankle, and was a member of various local guilds
and institutes. She was also an Olympic-grade fundraiser who
put her excellent singing voice to good use in raising money for
the construction of the Holy Trinity Church at Arowhenua. The
motives behind Ellen Foxon's involvement in this project — or,
more precisely, the motives Marguerite attributes to her and

to which we get shortly — now serve as the moral foundation on which Marguerite is basing her own part in the refurbishment of that same church. Ellen Foxon continues to shape events playing out some 90 years or so after her fundraising heyday.

Not only did William Green swim some cattle ashore on arrival at Akaroa, but he also occupied the house in which Te Tiriti o Waitangi was signed by two Ngāi Tahu rangatira on 30 May 1840 and, according to Joe's family lore, raised the British flag at Point Britomart up north (although no one seems able to confirm this).[19] William is also said to have fathered the first Pākehā child born in the area.

Bridget Kelly is unquestionably a big character in the history of the Ōpōtiki Kellys, but when last we encountered her she was in a fix. Recently widowed and mother to seven children, the sum of the support she received from the state following her husband's drowning was a month's rations for the family. (No military pension for Bridget.) But she made it through, purchasing land of her own in town and becoming one of two midwives servicing the Ōpōtiki area, receiving a guinea for bringing a child into the world and helping out with housework and cooking after the birth. Bridget died in late 1916, a grandmother to 79 grandchildren.

In some families people stand out for what they do. Dorothy and David's families provide a surprising number of senior members of the early police force.[20] Dorothy has done the legwork on this and found that 'McGrath, an Irish Catholic labourer, who appeared to be reasonably well educated, arrived in New Zealand in the 1870s. He joined the AC, served at Parihaka in No. 2 Company, and eventually became a Superintendent of Police.' She is pretty sure that he was not allocated land after the invasion of Parihaka.[21]

She is sure, however, of what happened to another ancestor, Browne, the 'well-educated son of an Irish lawyer'. His family 'had been dispossessed of their lands in Ireland and fought in European armies, where they collected titles such as Baron. Of the three sons, one stayed in Dublin, where he went into the Police Force and his two brothers went to Victoria, where they were also in the Police Force. The New Zealand Browne arrived in Hokitika in 1866 as one of the first detectives. He eventually became an Inspector of Police and when he retired, he became mayor of Melrose in Wellington.' (There is a small connection with my own family here; when my father was a baby he was admitted for a time to the Karitane Hospital in Melrose. I've never been able to find out why.)

John Bryce most certainly looms, and not just over Gillian's personal history. More than any of the other members of the colonial elite who angled for the invasion of Parihaka, her ancestor has come to embody the violation of the pā. Not only did Bryce participate in Te Pāhua but he also dismissed the 'supernatural *mana* of Te Whiti', upbraided Parihaka Māori as a people 'far gone in infatuation' for their leader, and suggested that while it was 'necessary to satisfy the Maori people that an inquiry should be made into certain Native grievances . . . he could not say that he attached the same importance to it as other people did'.[22] It cannot be comfortable to be a descendant of this man.[23]

There a link between Gillian's past and my own. Her forebear was central to what occurred on and after 5 November 1881; mine was there, too, but only to make up the colonial numbers. Still, it is a curious thing that Andrew Gilhooly was not much talked of in the wider family and I grew up knowing nothing about him. He was involved in one of the defining episodes of the colonisation of this country but left virtually no trace whatsoever in the family's collective memory. Philip Roth's notion of the 'blizzard of specific data that is a personal life' does not apply to Andrew Gilhooly.[24]

If anyone looms large in my family stories from that time it is Kate, Andrew's wife and my great-grandmother. She was born Catherine Fleming in Annah, Galbally, in County Limerick, in 1874. This was the year the man she would marry 23 years' hence and half a world away, who was 17 years older than her and from a neighbouring village, left Ireland for New Zealand. She was four when her mother died, and 21 when she migrated to the Cape Road along with her father, Richard, and three of her siblings, joining several half-brothers from her father's first marriage.

The Fleming name features prominently on the cadastral maps of the 1880s: between them, Michael, Richard and James eventually held title to 16 sections (totalling 394 acres, all confiscated land) clustered together towards the bottom of the Cape Road.[25] Kate joined her brothers on those maps in 1921, when she purchased Parihaka A. In her obituary she is recalled in warm, glowing terms, but the stories that have come down are of a dour, intimidating old Irish woman who browbeat her grandchildren (including my mother, who boarded with Kate for a couple of years) into endless rosaries, cups of tea and general misery. It didn't help that after her husband's death she required her sons to work on the family farms for wages — that still grates with my mother.

But while Kate — the last of the nine Flemings who had sailed from Ireland to die (in 1952) — is not fondly recalled, a grudging respect for her fortitude, strength of character and general doggedness persists. In a curmudgeonly, going-the-distance sort of way, she reflects well on us all.

*

But 'life hurls its blasts', and tucked in among the tales of hard slog, sporting derring-do and community service there is also tragedy.[26] Children die, their deaths chronicled if not foretold. In the stories shared with me, quiet places are still kept for the stillborn babies, drowned toddlers and fever-ridden youngsters. Families make and maintain room in their collective memory for those who died at war, under tractors, on gravel roads and at the bottom of rivers.

Susan alludes to a different kind of loss when she reflects that emigration usually meant that 'all extended family — aunts, uncles, cousins, grandparents, the lot, were left behind and, at that time with communication so limited and travel out of the question, never seen again'. (Not so for Win's mother, who was orphaned at the age of 12 and sent back to Scotland to be brought up by relatives, although you might not wish that on anyone.)

Our settler stories often leave little room for those who stayed at Home. Easy for me to see Andrew's voyage as the beginning of something new — but for the family who remained in County Limerick he may have been just one more 'lost strand in the plait of ancestry'.[27] Exile always extracts a price in this land where 'Christmas comes in summer, and other unexpected things may come to pass as well.'[28]

The tariff may be higher than we think, the weight of our settler stories leaving just the barest of spaces — a flicker at the margins — for the memory that, as Gillian puts it, once 'we came from something rather better than what has developed here, back in the place where we were native'. She is talking of a time before the Highland Clearances tore clans and communities apart, rent the ties between people and the land. But that is a lost place, long closed to us.

Nonetheless, Gillian recalls an attempt to leave this country and return to that one. In Ravenna, an ancient Byzantine city in the north-east of Italy, she 'dreamt this extraordinary dream' of an ancestress, 'a woman standing alone on a blasted heath, all her finery, her dress, hair, all tattered, distressed, and there's a castle burning in the distance, and she's standing at a kitchen bench, no house, no walls, just the bench on the heath, and she's peeling potatoes, and she turns to me and says, "Why have you come, why have you come? There's nothing for us here anymore. Go back."' So Gillian did, not even reaching the Scotland Highlands, 'where the ahi kaa is long cold'. Instead she quietly turned about and retraced her steps to a place at the bottom of the world where she feels 'betwixt and between. Neither here nor there.'

Māori paid a price, too, although our stories rarely make that apparent. Occasionally, of course, tangata whenua are right there in the mix, especially for those families such as Bridget Kelly's, with both Māori and non-Māori descendants. Sometimes, too, Māori appear as valiant adversaries. Win recalls her father 'being respectful of Māori and their knowledge of the land, bushcraft, rongoā. However, I also remember him saying that Māori were "beaten in a fair fight". Either he had grown up believing that, or it was an excuse for the reality.'

I do not wish in any way to diminish the fact or significance of these connections (and there are more later in the book): they are the 'give and take' that occurs on Alex Calder's 'ever-changing beach'.[29] Sometimes, however, it is as if Māori appear in our stories to make our own Pākehā ancestors look like good people. They are the support act to our lead role. One person I heard from was well aware that references to Māori in both 'the written and oral history tend toward [her] family members being helpful', such as the tales told of 'one of my grandfathers, a doctor, going out on horseback to remote Māori communities'.

There are, as well, stories of the friendships between Māori and Pākehā, and of ancestors — like Aidan's — who 'had very strong relationships with local iwi, and even learned to speak te reo Māori'. But from time to time I wonder if their purpose might not be to reassure us that, whatever occurred to them during peak colonisation, Māori bear us no ill-will now that 'everyone is the best of friends'.[30]

Often, though, Māori are not there at all. They are the absence that is always present, shunted aside by the bustling endeavour required to build a colony, put down roots, make a better life. As someone suggested to me, maybe that's because 'invisibilising Māori in the family story means that any injustices can remain unaddressed, which is [also] what happened in the country as a whole for a long time'.

3.
Standing in the Shade

F ROM A DISTANCE MOST THINGS LOOK BEAUTIFUL.[1] Our family chronicles are essentially secular creation stories, and therefore important for all the reasons such things matter: for the shape they give to the past, the justification they provide for the present and the direction they offer for the future. They are precious things — they contain whole families and need careful handling. But '[a]ll family trees are shady', and it is the shade, where the forgotten things lie, that I am most interested in.[2]

For one or two of the unsettled it is less a matter of coming to terms with what waits in the shade and more about learning to live with what is standing in plain sight. Gillian has always known about John Bryce, to whom she has ties through her father's side of her family. The Bryces were substantial landowners, and while '[w]e did not know the details of how that had come to be,' Gillian recalls, 'we did know that John Bryce was part of the government in the nineteenth century, that he had been involved with the wars against Māori and had led the invasion of Parihaka. We also knew of the libel trial in London, 1886, Bryce v Rusden, for he had published the transcript and there were one or two copies with the family.'[3]

The details of the Bryce story, however, were vague. We knew nothing of John Bryce's earlier life, that he had come out here as a six-year-old boy, with his father, older brother and sister; his mother had died of tuberculosis not long before they left Glasgow in 1839. They were an early part of the Wakefield colonisation scheme and arrived here in February 1840, days after Te Tiriti o Waitangi was first signed. After a few years of working as a carpenter, his father bought a small area of land in what is now known as the Hutt Valley, and though he [the father] did not join up with Governor Grey's militia to take part in the 1846 war, his older son, Thomas, did. There were atrocities committed then, too, the desecrations of pā and urupā amongst them; he took no further part in any more military actions after that, and a veil is drawn over that time.'

Gillian, then, lives with that which has never been forgotten. This is not something that can simply be achieved and set aside; this is a job of work that goes on and on. It is a constant companion. 'The main problem,' as she sees it, the thing that demands the most work, 'lies in those damages, an ancient way of life upended, the breaking of kinship bonds, the fracturing and scattering of people from their homes, their native lands, and their tūrangawaewae.'

For Gillian this is personal, and not just because one of her forebears played a central role in Te Pāhua o Parihaka. The destruction of community hits home because 'it is what happened to our own people in the old country when the clan structures were systematically broken, and it is still happening now: even the strength of my father's family has not been able to withstand these prevailing winds'. The common thread here is the malign influence of English imperialism, both in the Scottish Highlands and on the coast of Taranaki.

Jane's family has never really forgotten what lies beneath the family tree either, and for them there is also discomfort. 'My parents farmed in many places,' she writes, 'gradually increasing the size of their herd and the size of their farms. I was brought up on the Lower Puniho Road, last farm on the right, on West Coast lease land. My parents, especially my mother, were very sensitive and defensive about the status of this land. They also leased land around the Puniho Pā. I think they were relieved when they moved to the Waikato in 1973 leaving behind a political thorn.' (There are some thorns up there, too, but to the best of my knowledge farms on West Coast lease land are not among them.)[4]

The unease has been passed on. 'From my own point of view,' Jane muses, 'I feel very uncomfortable about the Taranaki history and my own family's role in that history, including the preferential rates charged for leasehold land at the time my parents were farming at Puniho. The only way I can deal with this is to accept that it happened and that the Treaty process is designed to address the manifest inequity created mostly in the nineteenth century.'

Jane is doing more than that. For one thing, she is facing the source of discomfort, not ignoring or turning away from it. Not everyone up that way does. She is also still asking questions. 'Why', for example, 'and how did the family get to be living "in the country" before the Taranaki wars? Did they buy?' She assumes so, 'because the phrase "driven from" their home indicates they felt they had some right [to the land]. From my father's comments I feel that the family had a strong connection to the land at Koru Road, Oakura, so maybe they had settled there originally.' But she cannot be certain.

Neither is Jane sure about the farm south of Ōpunake that her great-great-grandfather Frank (he of both sporting and musical prowess) moved to after leaving Koru Road in 1906. 'What was the origin of the Tangatara land?' she wonders. It is within the Taranaki confiscation line but she believes it may have been freehold land. Moreover, her people's 'relationship with local Māori was complex. Colonial attitudes prevailed but at the same time great friendships developed that endured a lifetime. My father's ashes are scattered on Taranaki maunga with approval from a kaumātua who had been schoolmates with David.' And her father's 'language at home was peppered with Māori words and phrases'.

What is more, Jane and her five siblings 'were taken to Parihaka and told of the appalling events'. Her brother Tim also remembers 'that my mother made sure that we knew about Parihaka, and as a family we knew [the invasion] was against all natural justice'. Even so, Jane continues, 'there was little discussion of land ownership regarding the farm at Puniho. I asked once and was peremptorily advised that "it's all perfectly legal". My mother felt that local Māori were overly demanding. By and large there was a code, perhaps unconscious, of silence. Friendships with Māori were discouraged.'

But of course they came about nonetheless: Tim's first friend was 'a boy called Loyden who lived with the Ngāwhare family down the Komene Road'. Mostly, though, Tim 'can really just recall a lot of hard work, including my mother doing a lot of manual work, like milking. There was certainly no sense of taking advantage of anyone. I do remember disparaging comments about weed-infested properties and statements that it was "Māori land". My memory is that there was just no connection between Māori people's economic circumstances (generally not great) and the history of colonisation throughout my upbringing — in my home or at school.'

*

You can sense these people's unease about the provenance of the places they grew up on; about what happened so that the land could become 'theirs'. The history of the West Coast Settlement Reserve lease system is particularly troubling. I referred to a couple of its key features in the opening chapter, including that from the early 1880s leases were administered on behalf of Māori landowners by a Crown official, and that many Māori were charged occupation licences (which sometimes exceeded the rents paid by Pākehā farmers) to inhabit their own whenua.

What I did not explain is that rents were determined by the public trustee, not by the land's owners, and were consistently set at peppercorn levels. Moreover, leaseholders could mortgage, sub-let or transfer a lease to other farmers regardless of owners' preferences, and could borrow money from the government to improve the land (a right that was not extended to Māori landowners).[5] And the passage of the West Coast Settlement Reserves Act 1892, of course, gave rise to perpetual leases.[6]

The point of the West Coast Settlement Reserve lease system was to prise Māori from their land. And it worked. By 1912, 60 per cent of the 193,996 acres set aside for native reserves in Taranaki had been leased to settlers.[7] By the mid-1990s, over 70 per cent of the land promised in reserves had been sold. That land is not coming back to Māori any time soon.

It isn't as if the malign nature of the system has gone unnoticed. As early as 1907 a commission of inquiry politely stated the obvious when acknowledging that 'the concentration of control [of Māori land] in a Department not in close touch with the Maori beneficiaries and their needs, whose paramount duty is to secure revenue from every part of the estate vested in it, is not always in the interests of the Maori beneficiaries, and is distasteful to them'.[8]

Since then, a string of public inquiries — the 1948 Myers Commission, the 1975 Sheehan Commission, the 1991 Marshall Review Panel — have reached much the same conclusion. And still this very particular type of arrangement endured. All the way up until 1997, when the Maori Reserved Land Amendment Act 1997 finally phased in market rentals and reduced the rental review period from 21 to seven years. And retained perpetual leasing.

Growing up on Māori land will tend to keep the disquiet to the fore. So will a family connection to someone as historically significant as John Bryce. But there is always work to be done, salvaging the things — Australian-Indian writer Kavita Bedford's 'dark shapes' — that have been lost in the weeds around the family tree.[9] It is discomforting, this particular kind of labour, not least because it finds expression in the realms of both the profane and the sacred.

Kiaran's great-grandparents, Andrew and Honora, 'came out from Ireland in 1875 on the *Edwin Fox*. They didn't meet on the ship but later on, and were married in Whanganui in 1877. They farmed at Rowan Road, Kaponga.' The Kaponga farm was one of half a dozen or so held in trust at the time Kiaran's parents moved onto it in 1956, but it was 'only after I returned to New Zealand and had done some reading', he goes on, 'that I realised that all of the properties that Andrew and Honora owned were on confiscated land. This fact really has been swept under the carpet and a lot of my aunts and uncles were uncomfortable about it. I remember asking what Andrew did during the Tītokowaru uprising and was told that "as he was a Catholic he wasn't allowed to bear arms but that he looked after the military's horses". Which I found hard to believe.'[10]

I am entirely with Kiaran on this small matter of religious camouflage. I was also raised a Catholic and am pretty sure there is nothing in the Good Book that would have threatened Kiaran's great-grandfather with the eternal fires of damnation if he didn't stick to feeding the horses of the blokes doing the fighting. But the anecdote reveals just how enduring the discomfort could be. It is unlikely to be a coincidence that the old people in Kiaran's family told this story about their ancestor's role in the colonial government's struggles with the great Ngāruahine rangatira.

The imperative to do well to others (or at least not to do them harm) lies deep in the Catholic psyche. Moreover, we Catholics are raised knowing that there is a price to be paid for behaving badly: it is terrible, terrifying and likely to hurt a great deal. So this story was an amulet. It kept the souls of Kiaran's aunties and uncles safe; held the threat of the fires of hell at bay.[11] This is no small matter and not to be scoffed at. But the point is that they have to keep on telling it. For ever. Their eternal souls depend upon it.

In John's history of his wife's ancestors there is no palpable threat to spiritual wellbeing, but unease is running beneath its surface nonetheless. Shortly after John Kelly arrived in New Zealand from Melbourne in 1864 he found himself in the Commissariat Transport Corps. The corps, which was under the control of the Imperial army rather than the colonial government, was at the logistical heart of the campaign in the Waikato. (It had also taken the lead in the construction of the Great South Road, which enabled the invasion to take place, although the war was well under way by the time John Kelly arrived.)

Kelly's movements during the war are hard to track (the labours of privates tending to be outshone by the endeavours of higher ranks), but John can place him in the contingent of militia and corpsmen sent to cut the supply route established over the Kaimai Ranges by Waikato Māori.

Kelly was in Tauranga, then, for the assault in late April 1864 on Pukehinahina Gate Pā, where the 500 Māori defenders were outnumbered eight to one but still managed to deal the British one of the biggest defeats of the New Zealand Wars.[12] John's sense is that as a member of the Transport Corps it is unlikely that Kelly took an active role in the fighting. Whatever the case, he soon moved on, attached to the 1st Waikato Militia dispatched as part of a larger military force to 'pacify' the Ōpōtiki region following the hanging of the Anglican missionary Carl Völkner by members of the Pai Mārire faith in March 1865.[13]

For a pithy description of the consequences of that action for mana whenua, Whakatōhea, it is hard to go past the recollections of Major St John, the commander of the Waikato Militia, who in later years would recall that '[v]engeance was taken; an expedition of colonial forces was sent to attack the murdering tribe; and, after losing heavily in men, the Whakatōhea were driven off their ancestral patrimony, which was given over to military colonists.'[14]

John Kelly was one of them. The nature and extent of his role in the reprisals taken against Whakatōhea remain unclear, although John supposes that, at the very least, Kelly, as a member of the Transport Corps, 'was part of the taking of Whakatōhea food and possessions'. What is known is that in early 1867, a year after he purchased a 1-acre block in Ōpōtiki town, Kelly took possession of Lot 99, the 50-acre block he might well have imagined years earlier in far-off Melbourne; it was part of the 114,000 acres of Whakatōhea land confiscated following Governor George Grey's 'proclamation of peace' in 1865. But I suspect that, from his wife Bridget's point of view, whatever this land may have represented (and she was to sell it eight years later for £25), it was overshadowed by her husband's drowning in the Waioeka River a matter of weeks after it entered her family's history.

War in the Waikato; Pukehinahina Gate Pā; the campaign against Whakatōhea; confiscated land. John's meticulous account of Kelly's small story is a doozy, and it seems he knew none of it before he sat down and started work.[15]

'There were definitely things that were left out' of Justine's backstory, too, including that her 'Pākehā ancestors had fought in the Land Wars, both in the Waikato and around the Gisborne area; the details of the purchase of a large piece of land by my great-grandparents in the Taranaki area in the late 1800s, especially how this land had become available for settlement; the role of my ancestor in assisting the New Zealand Company and the consequences their activities had for Māori; and the contribution my family made to the destruction of the ngahere [the bush] at the top of the Coromandel.' Those things, which have come to light only recently, also bother her mother, Win.

Aidan has his own silences to confront. While neither he nor his immediate family 'knows of any direct involvement in or benefit from conflicts and land confiscation, it's almost certain that there is more that we do not know'. Aidan is almost certainly right, because the dairy farm his grandparents ran, and on which his mother and her three siblings were raised, 'is a short walk from Te Ngutu-o-te-Manu', once home to Riwha Tītokowaru, and although it 'was purchased from another Pākehā family, considering its location it is beyond all doubt that this land would have been confiscated at some stage of the conflicts inflicted by the colonial government on the tangata whenua of south Taranaki'.

Marguerite is undergoing a similar process of excavation. Until recently, her understanding was that her people's time in Aotearoa began with her grandparents in 1906. They were from Leicester, and after arriving in South Canterbury farmed at Saint Andrews, lived in Winchester and retired to Temuka. She knew her grandmother had been active in St Peter's Anglican Church in Temuka, and that she was a keen croquet player. That was about the extent of it — until it wasn't.

Recently Marguerite has been asking probing questions about her ancestors and receiving some unexpected answers. For one thing, it seems they arrived in South Canterbury in 1908, not 1906, and that for a time they owned and operated a business combining billiards, hairdressing and tobacco. More significantly, it transpires that in addition to the farm in Saint Andrews, they had owned two other South Canterbury farms. That came as a bit of a surprise.

As she recalls, 'I started with PapersPast, and plugged in "Foxon", "1906" and "1947" — when my granddad died — and up came 3000 references. I spent three weeks trawling through these . . . and that's what suddenly opened my eyes: "Hang on a minute, there was more than one farm." Because I read things like: "Farewell at Winchester, the Foxons are returning to their farm at Epworth." Really, I thought? Where's Epworth? So I discovered they had the Saint Andrews farm, the Epworth farm and the Winchester farm.'

I read Marguerite's account and wonder how two entire farms could have been misplaced from the family memory — but then I recall just how much my own family had forgotten. Removing motes from your own eyes, and so forth.

Intriguingly, Marguerite also found that her grandmother, Ellen, had been involved with a second church, this one at the Arowhenua Pā, the major Māori kāinga in South Canterbury and just a couple of klicks out of Temuka. It is this relationship that Marguerite lingers on longest, because Ellen 'established the Māori Ladies Guild there in 1929, and was president for its first four years. In 1928, the Māori church, built in 1866, was in dire need of replacement. Efforts had been made over the years to raise the money to build a new church in the pā [but] funds were short and no work could be considered until they were in place.'

Within three years the guild members, who met monthly in the Foxons' farmhouse at Epworth, had raised the required amount — including through the sales of handiwork, sweets and fancy goods at stockyard sales, where special stalls would be set up (and following which dances might be held) — and the Holy Trinity Church at Arowhenua was consecrated in 1932. When Ellen moved away in 1934, Marguerite reports, one of the local papers noted that '[t]he Rev Mountford expressed regret at the departure of Mrs Foxon, who had founded the [Arowhenua] Guild, which had been instrumental in the building of the new Holy Trinity church at Arowhenua.' The reverend then asked

The first of these photos, taken in the early 1930s by William Anderson Taylor, shows the Holy Trinity Church built at Arowhenua Pā, near Temuka, in 1866. The second is of the 'new' Holy Trinity Church towards which Ellen Foxon's considerable fundraising efforts were directed, and which was consecrated in 1932.

Canterbury Museum Collection, Ngāi Tahu Archive, 1923.213.85; Marguerite Foxon, 2023

Marguerite's grandmother to accept a 'handworked Maori tea cosy' as a token of thanks. Mrs Rehu, from the Māori Women's Institute, gifted Ellen Foxon two flax kete.

You can see why some of this might be unsettling. Marguerite explains that when she first came across references to her grandmother's role in the Arowhenua Māori Ladies Guild, 'I thought it was ironic that she, a Pākehā, was president of a Māori organisation on one of the last tracts of land Ngāi Tahu held in the South Island. I felt something between being embarrassed that once again it's the "whites" who, in their arrogance, always step in to lead things, and a sense of being upset that she had somehow intruded into this Māori organisation.' Those sentiments sharpened when it became apparent that in the early 1930s Ellen had also been involved with the Arowhenua Māori Women's Institute, the first branch of that organisation to be established in Te Wai Pounamu.[16]

But resist the urge to judge and another type of meaning is possible. 'As I learned what was going on at the time in relation to trying to fund the rebuilding of the church, her on-going role in the guild and institute, and the outcomes of her leadership,' Marguerite continues, 'I feel proud that she took this on. For me it gives a sense that in a roundabout way my grandmother made a tiny contribution towards "atoning" for the fact that she and her husband had profited through their farms, all of which were on former Ngāi Tahu land.'

If you don't know what happened to Ngāi Tahu (and I didn't until I met Marguerite), a brief primer may be useful. Across a 20-year period in the mid-nineteenth century the Crown made 10 major purchases from Ngāi Tahu.[17] Thereafter, the iwi sought redress from the Crown for the unfair ways in which these purchases were undertaken. Those 10 acquisitions amounted to 34.5 million acres of land — roughly half of the land mass of the entire country — for which the Crown paid just £14,750 (about $2.5 million in today's money, which is the price of a modest place in Tāhuna Queenstown). For the whole of the South Island.

Furthermore, the Crown also breached its various deeds of purchase, including by failing to set aside in reserves 10 per cent of the land it had bought. In the entire Kemp Block, for instance, which encompassed roughly 20 million acres, just 6359 acres — 0.031 per cent of the total acreage — were reserved for Ngāi Tahu.[18]

All of this (and more) is set out in the Preamble to the Ngāi Tahu Claims Settlement Act 1998, which makes for depressing and distressing reading. The Preamble also includes references to legislation such as the Middle Island Half-Caste Crown Grants Act 1877, which made it lawful for the governor 'to execute Crown grants of such portions of the waste lands of the Crown situate[d] within the Provincial Districts of Canterbury and Otago . . . in satisfaction of any promise as aforesaid to any half-caste claimants . . . [p]rovided that the area so granted shall not exceed ten acres to each male and eight acres to each female'. This at a time when the minimum viable piece of land for a Pākehā farmer was considered to be 50 acres — at least that's what the Canterbury Lands Act 1851 stipulated. So, small scraps of waste land for the 168 people named in the legislation, and even those only because there was a non-Māori in their family mix.

Marguerite suspects that the shadow of this history lies behind her grandmother's efforts with the Arowhenua Māori Ladies Guild and the Māori Women's Institute. She does her due diligence and finds that many of the men involved in 'fighting with the government and talking with Apirana Ngata and the Land Court' had the same names as the women her grandmother knew at the guild and the institute.

Marguerite also stumbled across a photo of Wikitoria Paipeta, the first president of the Arowhenua Māori Women's Institute and the wife of Pita Paipeta, a key figure in the Ngāi Tahu campaign. Wikitoria Paipeta was the granddaughter of the religious leader Te Maiharoa, who in 1877 established a settlement near Ōmārama to protest the Crown's failure to honour the terms of the 1848 Canterbury Purchase.[19] As a descendant of Te Maiharoa, 'Wikitoria Paipeta had considerable mana and was deeply respected by the Judge of the Native Land Court, where she periodically appeared', Marguerite tells me. 'Ellen Foxon would have known her well from her involvement with the institute. This drives home to me again that my grandmother absolutely knew about and had to be immersed in the land issues facing these women she was mixing with. It would have been a regular point of discussion when they met.'

You can appreciate why it is taking Marguerite some time to work through all of this. There are many contradictions to be sifted. As we have talked over the last year or two, it has become clear to me that Marguerite is articulating the ambiguity of the descendant who can find much to admire in the actions of a forebear while also holding on to her discomfort with the circumstances and contexts in which those things took place.

She is doing an Elizabeth Strout: not indulging in 'a sorry shake of the head at the inadequacies of our settler forebears', but trying to sift, weigh and sort things that pull in different directions.[20] It's an example worth following.

✻

In the stories I grew up with about my mother's people, cows, rugby, farms and the Catholic Church feature heavily. So do baking, ample aunties, men who slept off the Sunday roast while the womenfolk did the dishes, and dances in country halls that have long since been shuttered.[21] What did not make the cut were some of the particulars about the farms that were harnessed to my family's history in 1895, 1902 and 1921 respectively. Time they did.

In late November 1895, Andrew paid £350 for Section 44 Block 12 of the Cape Survey District, a 114-acre piece of land adjacent to but on the seaward side of the South Road. (Contra the payment of the equivalent of a penny an acre for Ngāi Tahu land, in Taranaki the Crown didn't even bother to pay for the land that my great-grandparents farmed — it just took it.) He returned to Taranaki to take up the farm following a decade or so away, part of which was spent at Port Chalmers serving as a gunner in the newly formed Permanent Militia.

Seven years later, married now to Kate Fleming, he took out the lease on Section 103 Block 13 Cape Survey District, which is on the Opourapa Road.[22] Finally, on 31 August 1921, not a year before her husband died, Kate bought the 98-acre Parihaka A farm for £2947.

Pull the curtain back and the colonial shades start to gather. The first is obvious but bears repeating: each of those farms was on land confiscated from mana whenua. The Crown has repeatedly acknowledged that this land was taken from Māori through a series of actions which were 'indiscriminate in extent and application, wrongful and unjust, and were in breach of the Treaty of Waitangi and its principles'.[23]

The severing of the centuries-old tie between that land and its inhabitants through a legal fiction is repugnant. It is made worse by the casual, almost offhand expediency of some of the actions of the colonial administration and its functionaries. For instance, in an extraordinary act of myth-making and self-justification, in 1882 the Crown decided to hold back a further 5000 acres from any future reserves that might be set aside for Māori as 'an indemnity for the loss sustained by the government in suppressing the . . . Parihaka sedition'.[24] Those 5000 acres included the Opourapa Road farm and Parihaka A.

Moreover, Section 103 was trapped in the West Coast leasehold system, and as such its Māori owners could not negotiate leases or borrow money from the government to improve their land (although Pākehā farmers could, just as they could mortgage, sub-let or transfer a lease to others). Neither could Māori hope to get back on their land anytime soon, because after 1892 people like my great-grandfather held their leases in perpetuity.

In Taranaki — as in the Waikato, Ōpōtiki and elsewhere — the family farm is about as neutral and benign as the South Road, the lighthouse and the telegraph. Which is to say, not at all.

I am far from alone in stumbling across this sort of stuff well on in life. Win is 75 and, like John, has only 'recently learned my great-grandfather was recruited in Melbourne to fight in the Land Wars with land grants being offered on discharge'. None of this was talked about when Win was young. She grew up knowing only that Benjamin Johnson 'was an insurance agent, auctioneer, grocer and land agent in Hawke's Bay, then Coromandel'. As it happens, there was rather more to him than that.

before he became what she knew him to be, he had fought
under Lieutenant-Colonel Marmaduke Nixon, whose 200-
strong cavalry — 'Nixon's Horse' — was part of the force that
invaded the Waikato in 1863. Win's great-grandfather fought
at Rangiaowhia, where Nixon led the charge on a building
in which those defending the Ngāti Apakura village — an
unfortified, open place of respite for women, children and
elderly men — had taken refuge. Nixon was shot during the
assault (and would later die of the wounds he sustained),
and his troops reacted 'by killing Māori who attempted to
surrender or escape from the building, which was either set
on fire deliberately or ignited by sparks from musket fire'.[25]
The official account is that 12 Māori died at Rangiaowhia; Ngāti
Apakura say the figure was somewhere between 100 and 200.[26]

There is a revisionist argument, based on the description
of the building in which people were incinerated as a church,
and on the fact that both the Anglican and Catholic churches
in Rangiaowhia were still standing after the Waikato War,
that those burnings never occurred. But as Vincent O'Malley
points out in *Voices from the New Zealand Wars He Reo nō ngā
Pakanga o Aotearoa*, when Ngāti Apakura refer to a 'whare
karakia', they may be alluding either to a Christian church or
to some other place of religious observance in which non-
Christian forms of worship take place.[27]

O'Malley also includes four extended accounts of what
occurred at Rangiaowhia from people who were there. Each
one confirms that houses in which Māori had taken refuge were
deliberately torched. One of these was penned by Forest Ranger
Gustavus von Tempsky (who was not notably sympathetic to
the Māori cause): 'The house is one mass of flames, it is near

falling, when another Maori bursts from it, gun in hand — and drops, pierced by bullets while dauntlessly aiming at the foe. As he fell, the timbers of the roof bent inwards, the house tottered, and with a crack, crumbled to pieces on the well fought ground. Seven charred bodies of Maories and the first Defence Corps man were found amongst the blackened remains.'[28]

Win's great-grandfather received his land on discharge, but by 1879 he had sold it and the family had moved on. In Win's memory, however, 'there was never any mention of a land grant', nor any talk 'of the source of the original ownership of the land farmed'. But now that these matters have surged into view, she is 'deeply unsettled by the fact that my great-grandfather came here to fight' and 'was probably a brutal soldier fighting innocent people to gain land that was rightfully theirs'.

Seven decades into her life, she finds herself — alongside her daughter, Justine — confronting the fact 'that my forebears owned land and prospered as a result of colonisation, either directly or indirectly'. In my experience, once these sorts of challenging details have announced themselves, they tend not to fade away. But they can lie there — lost or perhaps simply waiting to be found — for a very long time.

4.

How to Forget

THE THINGS JOHN, MARGUERITE, WIN AND others of us now know to be true had to be recovered from the shady bits beneath our family trees. And it is no mystery why they might have wound up there, given the shuffling of feet, clearing of throats and general shiftiness they occasion when they are dragged back out into the light. They are not always welcome, these unlooked-for orphans of our family histories.

One way in which difficult stories can be forgotten is simply to change the subject and talk about something else. In the last couple of years I've heard from people who are 'sick of the pakeha bashing', who feel they are missing 'out on employment, grants, and support for being pakeha' and who appear to believe that 'Maori lives have improved from European invasion whether you admit it or not.' (For the record, I don't admit it, because I cannot see how having your whenua taken or purchased under the threat of military action, your language suppressed and your very existence in your own land called into question improves Māori lives.)

In much the same vein it has also been suggested to me that '[t]he closing down of the illegal Parihaka commune attained present-day visibility through a 1954 book by Pakeha Communist, Dick Scott [which was] a marathon piece of special pleading carefully crafted by a white Communist to foster racial discord.'[1] And I have been accused of wilfully ignoring that: (a) 'in 1840 New Zealand was populated by numerous tribes of subhuman cannibal savages', (b) the nation is undergoing 'an endless expansion of group rights to brown supremacist New Zealanders' and (c) the term Pākehā is a 'racist slur'.

There's plenty of this sort of comment to be found in a country where hackles (and other things) are raised when it is politely suggested that racism really is an issue here. That much was made strikingly clear when, in preparation for a lecture, I dived into the submissions made on the parliamentary petition prepared in 2015 by Waimarama Anderson and Leah Bell, students from Ōtorohanga College, which hoped to 'raise awareness of the New Zealand Wars and how they relate to local history for schools and communities; introduce these local histories into the New Zealand Curriculum as a course of study for all New Zealanders; and memorialise those who gave their lives on New Zealand soil with a statutory day of recognition'.[2]

I've done plenty of beetling around in parliamentary submissions and I do not recall having read comments like some of those expressed by the opponents of Anderson and Bell's petition. Barry, for example, reckons that 'Waimarama Anderson and Leah Bell tell lies about NZ history. The so-called "land wars" were in fact punishments of Maoris for repeatedly breaking the law and for rebelling in various ways against the law. This is the truth.'

Historical revisionism also bothers Rick, for whom the real problem is that 'New Zealand is being ruined by the deceitful rewriting of history by elite Maori and those who seek to change the facts in exchange for money'. I'm not sure that history of any sort much bothers Garry, who simply thinks that '[t]here were no New Zealand land wars'.

Charles tells us, 'The gravy train that has become maori reluctance to actually become educated and contribute to society is dragging this country down into the level of third world status and with it, our true historical past for a very minor and irrelevant majority of half castes determined to cherry pick the parts of their ancestry that bring the most pecuniary gain and an inflated and hugely undeserved self-esteem.'

In similar fashion, Dianne 'opposes this petition as it is simply another way for the pseudo Maori to create divisiveness in New Zealand', while Graeme makes it very clear that he 'OPPOSE[s] the Petition of the Brainwashed and Naïve Anderson and Bell to install a Public Holiday to perpetrate a Grievance Day to further indoctrinate gullible NZers to believe Rebels and Rebellions are worthy of Compensations'.

John and Hanneke 'are absolutely opposed to this nonsense about a special commoration day for the "Land Wars". Where is our much vaunted democracy when gutless governments are continually favouring these continuous outrageous manoeverings by "Maori" braying for special treatment and which present such unacceptable threats to this priceless paradise which every one of us should be priveleged to share with total equality.'

Jeffrey continues the slightly frantic tone: 'If the point of the day is to celebrate the colonial troop & loyal Maori who fought to up hold law and order against the rebels and terrorists that wanted to continue the traditional culture of warfare, cannibalism, slavery, rape, murder, utu and general mayhem then I'm all for it because we should celebrate the triumph of good over evil.' Cannibalism is a bit of a theme. Neill and Lorraine rather like the idea of 'a day called "Maori cannibalism Day"' and Pamela is keen on seeing 'compensation for all the Europeans who were subjected to cannabalism!'

Karen frets about 'the maorification of everything', as does Michael, who thunders that the 'Maori-isation of New Zealand and re-writing of our history goes on unabated and non-Maori have had enough!' More of the same is forthcoming from Mr Burge who is, frankly, 'sick of Maori hand out and they must be treated the same as everyone else in New Zealand. After all the maoris have been given way to much and have more money and assets then huge companies. I have been told they are the richest group in NZ which I believe. I am sick of hearing how hard done by they are and our kids must learn it at school.'

Thomas concedes that Māori 'are mostly good people', but then ruins things by suggesting that they need to 'accept the fact they are a thousand times better off since coming under Queen Victoria's rule than if they were never colonized by Britain. The French would have wiped them out most likely and failing that they would have suffered terribly under their pagan short life spanned and cannibalistic lifestyle.'

An awful lot of people insist it is simply time to move on.

They rattle me, these words, for their callous ignorance and furious refusal to accept that colonisation is not synonymous with civilisation for all. (They also rather make the case, if unwittingly, for the outcome the Ōtorohanga College students sought and eventually achieved.) There is a strange echo of the imperial age in this collective venting of spleens, as if these people believe that the historical forces that carried their forebears to this place were both benevolent and inevitable.

The British Empire has long since collapsed as a military, economic and moral project, but it is clear that some of the ideas that were at its core — the scientifically illiterate idea of 'racial' hierarchies and the ethically self-serving notions of 'civilising missions' — linger on. You can see, then, why people's hearts and minds matter as much as do land and governance.

The standard litany of allegations levelled at those who question the orthodox settler-colonial narrative includes the notion that it demonstrates a lack of respect for the hardworking pioneers who made this country — and who, in any event, were not personally responsible for colonisation any more than are their descendants. That stuff belongs elsewhere and with others. The penultimate point is usually that people should leave the past where it belongs and move on. And this suggestion is nearly always followed by a solid dose of 'what aboutism?'

Three of the most common 'what abouts?' are: (a) What about the Musket Wars?, (b) What about Māori cannibalism? and (c) What about all the good stuff the British did and brought?[3] (There's often a fourth, of course: What about Australia? Trudie Cain, a friend and fine sociologist to whose views on these matters I listen carefully, points out that this is the kind of question you ask if you want to create a hierarchy of racism in which New Zealand looks better than Australia — or in which the Australians have 'real' racism while we have the best race relations in the world.)[4]

'What aboutism?' is like a weird form of historical multiple choice in which the correct answer is never one of the options. It is also, of course, another tactic for deflecting attention from unpalatable truths and silencing people who ask awkward questions. It amounts to a refusal to countenance that the past that needs to be left behind was anything other than A Very Good Thing — effectively denying the experiences of those for whom it was, in fact, A Very Bad Thing. This is language being used to silence.

A lengthy quote from Rachel Buchanan's book *Te Motunui Epa* makes the point eloquently:

> You've signed a Treaty and now you're in like Flynn.
> It's time to subdivide, build some new streets and
> houses, telegraph lines and so on — but the original
> owners refuse to budge. What a pain! But there is
> a way around the impasse. A civilised way. Call it
> civilised. Say that word. And also say civilisation. Say
> Westminster. Point out that the other way is savage.
> Keep using that word. Savage. Add other words to it.
> Say violent. Also, seditious. Chuck in uncivilised while
> you are at it. They are all excellent words, use them
> often. Say rebels. Keep talking and pass another law.
> And another. It feels good. Keep going. Law, law, law.
> Fend them off. Knock them down. Lock them up.
> Burn their houses. Destroy their crops. Bomb them.
> Lawful. Right.[5]

The most polite thing I can say about the sentiments expressed by some of those who opposed Waimarama Anderson and Leah Bell's petition is that they are examples of what British social anthropologist Paul Connerton calls 'forgetting through voice': attempts to smother one thing with another.[6] (Sometimes all it takes to smother is a single word. In the 1960 *Descriptive Atlas of New Zealand*, Parihaka was named Newall, after one of the AC officers involved in the arrest of Tohu Kākahi, Te Whiti o Rongomai and Hīroki on 5 November 1881.)[7]

The responses also illustrate what Rachel Buchanan has in mind when she observes that '[p]eople have to work hard not to know, not to recall, not to see, to be truly ignorant'.[8] We tend to think of forgetting as something that happens to us: it quietly sneaks up from behind without us really noticing. But forgetting of the sort I've just described — the loud clamouring of voices engaged in drowning out inconvenient truths by jamming one version of history down on top of another — is active, not passive; a practice people engage in rather than a process that happens to them.

'In one easy step,' says Gillian, reflecting on her own people's migration from the Scottish Highlands following the Clearances, 'we can forget the terrors and injustices of what had happened in our own countries, and also ignore the same things that happened to the people of this land. We can live in a disembodied present, apparently disconnected with anything of the past. It simply does not exist or have any bearing on our lives now.' Less about being careless, then, than about consciously expunging. And doing it over and over again, lest the forgetting end and the reckoning begin.

One of the specific ways of doing this — one of the diversionary tactics — is to frame attempts to end historical amnesia as disrespectful attacks on the dead. John is right in saying that you 'can't repudiate lives and events that are part of the history of [our] existence', but he is also correct in noting that it is perfectly possible to talk about what our Pākehā ancestors were caught up in without blaming them for those things. It's an important distinction, although one a significant chunk of public opinion refuses to accept.

Reluctance to examine the past can stem from a fear of learning what might lie there. But it can also reflect a concern that we might slip over into the 'complacency of hindsight' and place upon people long dead the impossible burden of knowing all future consequences of their choices and actions.[9] Or we might wind up doing something Keith Ovenden warns against: imposing the 'possibly false or the imaginatively inaccurate, free interpretation of motive and purpose' on others' lives.[10] He is right. Those lives are not subject to our direct understanding, for they have already been lived without us. We cannot access them, and so we can never fully know. The best we can do is interpret.

The historian Charlotte Macdonald also advises against indulging in the conceit of the present.[11] To do so is to erase ambiguity and context, and deny agency to those no longer capable of it. You can't simply say so-and-so thought this or that when you have no basis for doing so: recruiting the dead to your purposes by getting them to tell the story you want to hear from them is a distasteful thing to do.

I cannot deduce my great-grandfather's intent (or views on empire, Māori or anything else) from my contemporary understanding of the momentous happenings he was party to, any more than I can sensibly hold him responsible for all that colonisation has visited upon tangata whenua.

What is more, as Gillian wisely points out, those among our ancestors who left to escape the misery of Ireland or the poorhouses of industrial England 'arrived here already estranged from the old way of life [and] the vacuum in its place would have made fertile ground for the dominant ideologies of nineteenth-century imperialism, dividing the world into civilisation and savages, and hawking notions of the supremacy of the British races. Displaced and scrambling to find footholds in what was seen to be part of Britain, most had no idea that they had come to a Māori world. For the main story not told was that of the Treaty of Waitangi, much less of Te Tiriti o Waitangi; there was no awareness that we came to a place, and a way of life, which belonged with other people, and that we were here by the good graces of that agreement.'

I imagine that Ovenden, Macdonald and Gillian would concur with Elizabeth Strout, who is all in favour of 'coming to the page without judgement'.[12] It is helpful advice, and while it does not mean that everybody gets a free pass, it is a reminder of the risk of erasing the distinction between individuals and the broader sweep of the times they lived in. Of succumbing to the error, as John sees it, of reading 'the past as if the person knew the future'.

Which does not, of course, preclude seeking a more historically informed understanding of those pasts. Andrew Gilhooly could not possibly have anticipated the future consequences of his actions — but a century or so later I know some of them, and therefore can no longer hide behind him as a way of avoiding the issue. That point was made by a correspondent who wrote that although they were 'not personally responsible for the past I am a participant, as a member of a democratic state, in what happens now. I believe the most important thing we can do is acknowledge the past and our association with it. It is not an easy thing to do. It is not an easy thing for Māori to bear.' Quite.

It should be possible to engage in this kind of memory work without being derided or attacked for doing so. It is mendacious to conflate someone's attempt to understand their past with an act of judgement of those who inhabited that backstory. Adopt this position and we consign ourselves to an eternal present in Buchanan's 'dementia wing' of our history — which is a good way of dodging the tricky stuff, but no way to make sense of, much less come to terms with, a past that will never leave us.[13] (I've noticed that quite a number of people disagree with me on this point. These are often the same people who will encourage anyone lingering over our colonial history to 'move on', and who are quite happy to exercise a relativism — 'You can't judge your ancestors by today's standards' — that they resolutely reject in other contexts: 'After all, we're all one people'.)

When it comes to the dead it helps to hold two contradictory things in mind simultaneously. In my case that means balancing an understanding of the reasons my great-grandparents left Ireland with the perfectly reasonable intention of starting afresh in a new land with the knowledge that in building that new life they were part of a colonising project that blighted the lives of others. Put another way, and as Charlotte Macdonald also explains, you need to know your own history *and* be mindful of the risk of finding out that that past contains events that shattered the histories of others. For many of us, it is not possible to have one without the other.

Avoiding the issue is one way of forgetting, but you can achieve much the same result simply by not talking about things. As social anthropologist Carolyn Morris puts it, 'not-talking' about something leads to 'not-knowing' about it; and, eventually, a thing that is neither talked about nor known ceases to exist.[14] Morris's 'not-talking' is a way of 'sweep[ing] away all those traces that might show you where you have come from', which you might be especially inclined to do if they cast an unfavourable light on your backstory.[15]

As Win puts it, 'I think some things are probably intentionally forgotten because they might have meant that [people's] forebears were in the wrong.' In time those things, whatever they once were, simply drift away. Reflecting on why, as a younger person, she had not joined the family's historical dots together, Justine says, 'It all felt so long ago somehow, and not especially personal.' And it hadn't occurred to her to ask.

Nonetheless, what is not there may be every bit as consequential as what is — perhaps more so. This sort of forgetting is not accidental. Rather, it generally has a purpose, one which Gillian explains perfectly. 'I am inclined to think now,' she says, 'that the vagueness of the details is a useful thing; it becomes part of an assumption that this is how things work, and leaves untouched the machinery beneath it, the ways in which the original way of life is systematically destroyed. The stories that are told rest on that uneasy ground between knowing and not wanting to know, not-knowing, an indeterminate space.'

Neither is this really to do with loss, which is conventionally associated with forgetting. Forgetting the sound of a loved one's voice, or the texture of their skin or the way their face looked oddly back-to-front in the mirror — all these occasion a profound sense of loss. But when we forget the sorts of unpalatable truths with which this book deals — or leave them discarded in the half-light on Gillian's 'uneasy ground' — then we *gain* certain things.

In my case, not remembering meant that for 50 years I got to avoid having to confront the fact that my family shucked off its Irish tenant farmer identity and remade itself as a settler-colonial family on the basis of land that had been taken from other people. It meant I did not have to confront the paradox that my great-grandfather was born on Irish land that had been confiscated by the English and died in possession of whenua confiscated from Taranaki Māori. And it meant that I got to claim my part in the farmers-are-the-backbone-of-the-nation narrative without having to question where the farms in question came from.

More generally, for those of us descended from settler stock, not remembering means that we get to tell the pioneer story | get over it | be one people | move on | turn away. We are able to maintain the emotional and cognitive machinery keeping the entire confection in place — the 'apparatus necessary to its perception' — without acknowledging its existence.[16] In doing so, we engage in Paul Connerton's 'constitutive forgetting', which is the kind we reach for when we need to discard an earlier identity in order to create a new one.[17]

I think this notion rather neatly explains why so many of us continue to cleave to our pioneer shibboleths through a never-ending act of 'collective memory politics', and why any suggestion that we consider doing otherwise is liable to be met first with confusion, then with disbelief and finally with anger.[18]

We can also forget things we are looking straight at. Kiaran and his family 'would often go to Sunday mass at different locations' around the Kaponga area, 'depending on mass times and when milking was finished. One of the places we attended was Ōkaiawa, and on the way there we passed Te Ngutu-o-te-Manu, where there was a big AA sign saying that von Tempsky had been killed there, and that "no greater love hath a man than he lay down his life for his friends". As a kid I really wondered about this, but Dad didn't have any information other than that von Tempsky had died fighting the Māori.'

But focus on the Forest Ranger's demise and you miss what really happened on 7 September 1868, which is that Riwha Tītokowaru, the prophetic mission-educated Pai Mārire leader, handed a 360-strong government force a thumping at the pā he had established just six months earlier.[19] The 7 September sortie by Lieutenant-Colonel Thomas McDonnell's contingent of AC members, volunteers and Whanganui Māori was, in fact, the third assault launched on the pā in retaliation for an attack Tītokowaru had made on Turuturumōkai in July.

The first failed when the attackers got lost in heavy rain. The second fizzled out when they withdrew under heavy fire from the pā's defenders. The third ended in what James Cowan called 'a disastrous defeat for the Government column'.[20] Twenty-four of McDonnell's men were killed and a further 26 were injured. Three of Tītokowaru's warriors fell. The AC subsequently withdrew to Waverley and McDonnell was relieved of his command. More significantly, a colony was badly shaken.

All of this, but what most Pākehā know about that battle boils down to the death of one 'dashing colonial folk hero', immortalised in Kennett Watkins' political-colonial painting *The Death of Von Tempsky at Te Ngutu o Te Manu*.[21] And that most of the roads in the area are named after men — von Tempsky, Palmer, Hastings, Rowan — who were soundly defeated by Tītokowaru's forces. Kiaran remembers wondering about this, too; about why the names of the vanquished rather than those of the victors feature on the road signs.

Not far from Te Ngutu-o-te-Manu is the route I take each time I head back to New Plymouth to visit my mother and sister. Kiaran would know it well, as would Jane, Tim, Aidan and others with ties to Taranaki. It is a beautiful road, SH45, heading north out of Hāwera and swinging around through the coastal towns of Ōpunake, Rāhotu, Pungarehu and Ōkato before reaching New Plymouth. If you drive it on a clear day you can see the inverted parabola of the land as it swoops down from the summit of Taranaki maunga and gently levels off to blend into Te Moana-tāpokopoko-a-Tāwhaki, the Tasman Sea. Even on a bad day the mist and the wind will hint at that clean, clear line just behind the veil.

Not a lot of thought is given now to the history of the South Road. But the fact is that long before it delivered surfers to the ocean it delivered the AC to Parihaka.[22] It is an invasion road. The road's origins reach back at least as far as 1870, when there was a flurry of letters between Donald McLean, the native and defence minister, and Robert Parris, the civil commissioner in Taranaki, concerning a proposal '[t]o commence road works between Stoney River, and Waingongoro'.[23]

Making roads in Taranaki, and travelling on them, was hard work. F. A. Carrington, superintendent of the province of Taranaki, after whom the road that climbs out of New Plymouth up to the mountain is named, noted that the 'bush roads in Taranaki are good for cart traffic for about eight months in the year; during the rest of the year they are more or less soft and muddy'.[24] Nonetheless, by 1871 or 1872 a road constructed with the assistance of mana whenua Ngā Māhanga a Tairi ran from the bridge over the Hangatāhua as far as the Puniho corner.[25] At Puniho, it veered west towards the ocean until it reached the Waiorongomai Stream, where it eventually connected with the existing 'Native track seaward'.[26] (The track in question ran south around the coast from Waiorongomai to Umuroa, which is just north of Ōpunake and was, I learn from Kelvin Day, former tumuaki of Puke Ariki Museum in New Plymouth, the main kāinga of Wiremu Kīngi Moki Te Matakātea.)[27]

Only remnants of that old coastal route remain, but they retain their potency. Shortly after *The Forgotten Coast* was published I was told of a farmer from the Warea area who experiences 'an annual encroachment from [another] farmer at the bottom of Puniho Road who says he has access along the old Coast Road as a paper road to take his stock to winter grazing . . . it is an annual scrap!'

After a lull of nearly a decade — Te Whiti having refused to allow construction to push further south — and with the clamour for a resolution of the Parihaka 'issue' growing, work on the South Road began again in earnest in 1880. From the north, the original Hangatāhua to Puniho section was repaired, and a new road was forged south towards Parihaka along the route now followed by SH45. From the south the AC's road party — under the command of my great-grandfather's company commander, Major Forster Goring — pushed north from Ōpunake (the road through from the Waingongoro having already been completed at the cost of £1200, with substantial contracts going to Māori from Ōpunake, Oeo and Kaupokonui).[28]

I don't know exactly where the two roading parties came together to complete the invasion road, but I do know that when they eventually did it became clear that the road was closer to the mountain than its surveyors had originally planned — which meant that some 5000 additional acres on the seaward side of the road became available for purchase by Pākehā farmers.[29] (Confiscated land on the western side of the road was made available for settlement, while land on the mountain side was notionally set aside for Māori.)

The problem, it seems, was a reliance upon outdated maps: 'When we made our Interim Report, we could only conjecture where the new [South] road would be taken, and we did not then think there would be more than 10,000 acres of open country seaward of it. The line of forest had, however, been shown too near the sea in the old maps, and the road has been taken a straighter line than we thought likely. The result has been to cut through some Native cultivations: and . . . the area left for settlement thereby turns out to be 15,000 acres instead of 10,000.'[30]

The recommendation was that all of the 'Native cultivations . . . as well as any old pas or burial places, together with such fishing-places as it may be proper to let them keep at the mouths of any streams' within the 5000 acres that had been lopped off be kept aside for Māori. In the main that did not occur: the first of the three Gilhooly farms, Section 44 Block 12 of the Cape Survey District, is just one of many inside that 5000-acre band that quickly wound up in non-Māori hands. Some land was reserved for Māori, but most of it was alienated in the years ahead.

The point is that the South Road is not neutral. It is not any old road. At the time of the Great Famine in Ireland my great-grandfather's people 'built roads which went nowhere'.[31]

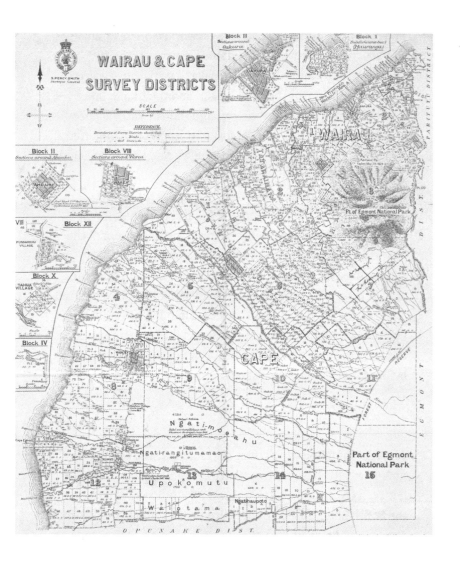

Prepared just four years after the invasion of Parihaka, W. Gordon's 1885 cadastral map of the Wairau and Cape Survey Districts illustrates the extent to which Taranaki has been sliced up into family farms. Tucked away at the bottom of Block 13 of the Cape Survey District, Parihaka sits in the middle of the last remnants of land yet to be fully 'sectioned'. *Puke Ariki, ARC2009-47*

This was not the case for the road he worked on in Taranaki, which was expressly built 'to enable a military force, if necessary, to be moved up to Parihaka'.[32] Its purpose was to sever the relationship between Māori and their land, first by conveying men carrying weapons and then by carrying people who came to farm the land.[33] Most of this has been forgotten, replaced by an eternal present in which people travelling along the South Road simply enjoy the view.

And it didn't take long for the amnesia to set in. Just three years after the invasion of Parihaka, the government congratulated itself on having 'secured the settlement of the country by Europeans to a very large extent', and on 'fast converting a wilderness, which five years ago was the home only of pigs and wild cattle, into cultivated farms, interspersed with numerous villages, and traversed in numerous directions by excellent roads'.[34] They remembered the pigs and the cattle, but had already forgotten the people who had been there long before the coming of the Pākehā.

The telegraph line which once ran alongside the South Road no longer intrudes on the vista. Telegraphic silence had lain between Ōkato and Ōpunake since 1873, but as the pincers of the South Road closed around Parihaka, so too did that 28-mile gap, the AC doing its bit not only by helping build the road but also by assisting the Telegraph Department's workers to 'erect and connect' the line, and by furnishing telegraph operators at its own road camps.[35]

Although the lines strung by my great-grandfather and his comrades have gone, the third leg in the trifecta, the

Cape Egmont lighthouse, is still very much there. The decision to erect a lighthouse at the bottom of the Cape Road appears to have been taken in late 1877, the expectation being that a 'very great political effect would be now produced upon the Natives throughout the coast if they saw the three things for which the Government [has] so long contended, being done together; the road, the telegraph line, and the lighthouse'.[36]

Major Brown, who had led the surveying of the Waimate Plains in south Taranaki, conceded that erecting the lighthouse 'would establish a raw place, if it was not viewed as a challenge [by mana whenua], as it probably would be'.[37] By 1881, the lighthouse at Mana Island having been dismantled and installed at Cape Egmont, the challenge had been laid down. The lighthouse loomed over the Cape, and over Parihaka, connected to the South Road by a small, 'roughly formed' secondary route '3 miles long and 30 feet wide'.[38]

The road, the telegraph and the lighthouse: a trinity of 'useful works' whose purposes were to intimidate and expedite invasion and settlement.[39] But the parts they played in the terrible things that happened in Taranaki in the late nineteenth century are now barely remembered by Pākehā — although mana whenua are reminded of them daily as they travel the road that ushered in the AC and alienation.

As you drive around the coast you see examples of other public constructions which perform the work of remembering certain things while forgetting others. Heading south, there are memorials to the two world wars in Omata (where, since 2019, the small memorial obelisk has listed the names of two men of German descent, George and Herman Bollinger, who were originally left off), Ōkato, Wārea (where the memorial plaques once held at the local school are now down at the Cape Egmont Boating Club), Pungarehu, Rāhotu and Ōpunake. They are among the thousand or so war memorials dotted around the motu commemorating the two world wars.

As far as I can tell, however, only 80 mark the New Zealand Wars. (Rachel Buchanan has a different take on this: for her, '[e]very block of Māori land in Taranaki is a war memorial'.)[40] Around the Taranaki coast, which those wars visited and left scarred, there is just one, on the Lower Pitone Road at Tātaraimaka, just south of Ōakura, which recalls the names of 28 Māori who were killed in the Battle of Katikara on 4 June 1863.[41]

The Katikara memorial, which was unveiled in 2002, was the outcome of a collaboration between mana whenua, Ngā Māhanga a Tairi, and the Ministry for Culture and Heritage. But the inscriptions on some of the older memorials to our wars often tell a quite different story from that recounted at Katikara. The one at Moutoa, in Whanganui (generally acknowledged to be the country's first war memorial), is not atypical in its dedication: 'To the memory of those brave men who fell at Moutoa 14 May 1864 in defence of law and order against fanaticism and barbarism'.[42]

Before the inscription was replaced in 1869, the memorial at Wairau, in Marlborough, was held 'Sacred to the Memory of twenty-two Englishmen, Who were murdered by the Natives of New Zealand on the 7th June, 1843'. Frequently Māori are not mentioned at all, although those who fought alongside the imperial regiments are sometimes acknowledged. These monuments are no more neutral public works than are the

Cape Egmont lighthouse or the South Road. Many carry out a selective labour of remembrance: gallant British valour commemorated; murderous Māori perfidy decried.

Accordingly, these memorials exercise people's emotions. 'I am very glad to see statues of colonial leaders being pulled down,' says 81-year-old Susan. 'Yes, we need to remember what these men did, and even make statues of them, but only to go into museums, not to be put on pedestals in public places so that we are obliged to look up to them.'

Susan tells me that she is well aware that when people 'look at me, a white woman', they make assumptions 'that are completely different from the assumptions [they would make] if I was Māori'. She entirely understands the work that those war memorials are performing, the way in which they inscribe in marble and in rock a particular interpretation of history. I rather suspect, too, that she has reflected on what they might mean for tangata whenua.

The oldest of my correspondents are the most emphatic on this matter. Win is even less equivocal than Susan: she would simply 'like to see all references — street names, town and city names, monuments — to those who drove, fought, confiscated, or perpetuated injustices, illegal land grabs and exploitation removed'. That would include, I suspect, the one you spot when driving through Ōtāhuhu in south Auckland. There, on the verge of a bustling road, stands 'a tall, narrow obelisk'.[43] The monument is a memorial to Marmaduke Nixon, under whose command Win's great-grandfather fought at Rangiaowhia, and the road is the Great South Road, built in the early 1860s to deliver an invasion force into the heart of the Waikato.[44]

The obelisk, which was constructed in 1868, acknowledges the sacrifice of the 'brave men who served their Queen &

Country' but makes no mention of those on the opposing side. Justine, Win's daughter, lives and works out that way, and I wonder what she thinks as she drives past this public tribute to a man who 'wasn't very nice to the Māori'.[45]

There is another type of public monument to the Age of Empire, far more numerous than those which attract Susan and Win's ire — but much harder to see. Gillian reminds me of this when she mentions that her 'Nana's great-uncle, William Goldie, known as a caretaker of Albert Park in Tāmaki Makaurau Auckland, in fact co-designed and planted the park when the Albert Barracks were no longer needed to house the colonial troops. He made the place into something more peaceable, but it was also a way of transforming it into a European space.'[46]

Which brings to mind sociologist Avril Bell's account of her own connection to Albert Park through her great-great-grandfather, George Graham, who oversaw the construction of the British Army barracks that once stood on that land, and to whom the initial idea for the park is attributed.[47] Many of the English oaks planted near Old Government House, which is adjacent to the site of the old barracks, are said to have grown from acorns that Graham arranged to have sourced from Windsor Park and delivered to the colony's governor. Acorns from Windsor: George would have been hard pressed to find another tree more emblematic of the British Crown.

What Gillian and my friend Avril are inviting us to consider is that the planting and nurturing of oaks and other exotic species by men like George Graham and William Goldie was part of 'the creation of the settler world, the project of re-making the "new" world in the image of the "old", of making the "new" lands homely, of "civilising" the "wilderness"'.[48] It occurs to me, now, that the phrase 'invasive species' is more accurate than I have hitherto appreciated. Not all monuments to empire, it turns out, are pointy and made of marble. Not all acts of colonisation require picking up a gun. And the oak trees in Albert Park are not neutral.

5.

The Forgotten Country

THE ORIGINAL REASONS FOR THE BUILDING OF roads, lighthouses and telegraph lines in Taranaki are not all that have gone missing. In my family's case, not only has there long been silence regarding Andrew, the AC and the confiscations, but much of what might have prompted my great-grandfather to leave County Limerick in 1874 seems also to have been forgotten. Ireland has been left behind in fact and in memory.

I have Eddie O'Dea to thank for the recovery of some of those memories. Eddie, a local historian from Kilteely, in the east of County Limerick, got in touch with me a year or so ago and offered to forward material on the Gilhoolys that he has gathered over the years.[1] As it happens, there is rather a lot of it — and it poses a whole new series of conundrums which I have come to think of as the Irish Paradox (and which sociologist Dani Pickering calls the 'Celtic Question').[2]

The paradox is not particular to me; it also applies to a good many other people whose families, having suffered at the hands of English colonisers, came to Aotearoa only to become colonisers themselves. But figuring this paradox out has got to be part of getting our small stories straight. My mother's family came from the west of Ireland. 'Gilhooly' is an anglicisation of the Gaelic Mac Giolla Ghuala ('son of the servant of Ghuala'), who were a sub-clan of the O'Mulveys, and originally from the Connacht counties of Roscommon and Leitrim. (There are records of at least three Gilhoolys who served as priests in County Leitrim between 1461 and 1505.) As far as I can tell (which really means as far as Eddie O'Dea can tell), my great-grandfather's branch of the Gilhoolys moved south from Connacht to Limerick at some point in the eighteenth century.

Andrew Gilhooly was born in 1855 in Ballynagreanagh — Baile Na Greine in the Gaelic — in the eastern reaches of the county. (The name can be translated as the 'Townland of the Sun', which seems a little optimistic given the nature of the Irish weather. Perhaps the village has a micro-climate.) Ballynagreanagh has an unsettled history reaching back to the English Commonwealth (1649–1660), when it was part of a large parcel of Irish land granted to the English brothers Daniel and Isaac Pennington.

Daniel was a London fishmonger, and disappeared into the miasma of seventeenth-century London. His brother is a different matter. Isaac was a Cromwellian adventurer, member of the House of Commons between 1640 and 1653, the mayor of London in 1642, one of the 135 commissioners of the High Court of Justice who tried Charles I in 1649 (although he did not sign the king's death warrant), and a member of Oliver Cromwell's government. Following the Restoration, Pennington lost those lands, as well as his life (he was arrested for high treason and died in the Tower of London on 16 December 1661), and in 1699 some 186 acres in and around Ballynagreanagh passed to the Duke of York.

By 1846 — three years after Andrew's father, Hugh, had moved from Ballinagally (the 'Town of the Nuns') to

Ballynagreanagh — the lands of the village were held by a John Massy of Barna, Galbally. (This, coincidentally, is the town in which Andrew's future wife, Kate Fleming, will be born in 1874, the year he left the country.) But Massy had leased the land — in perpetuity — to William Anderson, who lived in Devonshire and who in turn sub-let Ballynagreanagh to some 20 tenants at £2.14 per annum per acre. Hugh Gilhooly was one of them.

Evictions routinely took place in and around the townland, one of which was to have direct consequences for my great-grandfather. In 1833 a Michael Mahoney had been evicted from his land for non-payment of rent, and a man by the name of Kennedy was moved onto it — backed by the authority of the courts and the heft of the Irish Constabulary.

Life in Ballynagreanagh got off to a rough start for the Kennedys. The trouble — which it transpired was instigated by a very grumpy Michael Mahoney and one of his daughters — began shortly after the Kennedys moved in. On 3 September 1833 the front page of the *Newry Commercial Telegraph* reported:

> On Tuesday morning, a party of twenty-four men, under the command of Chief Constable Brady, proceeded to the lands of Ballynagrena, in this County [Limerick], with an intention of protecting property in corn, standing crops, etc., of a person named Kennedy, who held ground there, as tenant under the Courts, and who was not very long since put into the occupancy by the County Sheriff, with the aid of military force ... On the approach of Mr. Brady's detachment, they were fired upon by about twenty men, some of them protected by a high hedge, and

others by the walls of a farm house which had been burned by the persons opposed to Kennedy's interest, in June last. The assailants, after having firing, fled — they could not be overtaken, owing to the difficulty experienced by the Police in getting over the hedge, which was six feet high and covered with thorns. The fire was returned by forty-one shots by the Police … The police were all uninjured, but one of the others was, it is supposed, badly wounded. He was, however, carried off. The assailants wore neither shoes nor coats, and the surrounding hills were crowded with persons, who cheered the countrymen during the conflict!

Things did not much improve, and on 24 July 1835 the *Saunders's News-Letter* informs one and all that:

On Saturday last a dreadful affray took place in the lands of Ballynagreeanagh, near Kilteely. It will be remembered that these are the lands from which the sheriff and a party of police and military, some time ago, disposed the old tenants. One of the new tenants, named Kennedy, was, we understand, cutting down a boundary double ditch, which lay between himself and another man, named Power, who endeavored to prevent him. Blows ensued, and Power was severely handled; but his friends on hearing it having come up to his assistance, the battle became general, and one of Kennedy's friends having received a dreadful blow of a stone is despaired of. Kennedy's party had ultimately to retreat.

It was this man's daughter, Mary Kennedy, whom my great-great-grandfather Hugh married in 1843 in Kilteely church. By 1847, when starvation was laying waste to the west and the south of the country, he and Mary had taken over the lease to 28 acres of the land that Mahoney had been evicted from in 1833, and my great-grandfather was born on this wee skerrick of soil in 1855.[3] Whether or not his father required the protection of the Irish Constabulary is not recorded; neither is there any indication that Hugh and Mary suffered the same fate as had befallen the 'land-grabbing' Kennedys when they first moved into the neighbourhood.[4]

If there is some doubt over the reception Hugh and Mary received from their neighbours, there is no question that they suffered during the Great Famine. In early January of 1847, the year they took over the small farm on which they would, in time, raise 10 children, a General Hewetson received a letter from a subordinate, Lieutenant Ingles. On visiting Kilteely ('being wretchedly small and impoverished'), Ingles wrote, he had:

> found a population reduced to such utter and extreme destitution, with the prospect of daily increasing poverty, that I greatly fear, if their condition be not very shortly amended, wholesale starvation must ensue. Their position [is] one of imminent and extreme danger, and such is the position of very many families at the moment in the Kilteely Relief District. I have not, during the last 11 months in Ireland, witnessed such distress as in Kilteely on Tuesday last; and I have been a good deal through the western counties. [D]eath was too clearly depicted on

the majority of the countenances around my car in the street, and their cries too forcibly described their suffering. Such must be the state of things in a district where the proprietors of the soil are never seen and when provisions are beyond the reach of people.

It is a wonder that Andrew made it into the world at all. Less surprising is that, at 19, he chose to leave a land still in the shadow of famine.

At this point, I would like to veer off briefly into an aspect of Irish history I had been unaware of until Eddie O'Dea alerted me to it. It helps explain both why my great-grandfather left Ireland (as did several of his brothers, one heading to Boston and two others washing up in Hawke's Bay), and the choices he made here in New Zealand. By extension, perhaps it also speaks to the experiences of others who left that land for this.

For the better part of 200 years, gangs, or factions, engaged in acts of violence in streets, at county fairs and at horse races across Ireland. Pitched battles — fought to right wrongs, revenge earlier defeats, or to uphold the honour of a neighbourhood — might number tens or hundreds of men (and from time to time women) wielding reaping hooks, swords and shillelaghs (tempered staffs of hardwood, sometimes weighted at the top with a knob of iron to make them more lethal).[5] In Limerick, the most notorious factions were the curiously named Three Year Olds and Four Year Olds. Accounts of the names vary: some say they date from a long-forgotten dispute between farmers regarding the age of a bull (or it may have been a colt or a pig), while others argue that they refer to the length of time the rival faction leaders pledged to maintain their feud.

The Gilhoolys were prominent members of the Four Year Olds. In 1873 Michael Gilhooly — Andrew's first cousin, known in faction fighting circles as Fox — 'wheels' (that is, flourishes his blackthorn and shouts the battle-cry of his faction) in a fracas in the district of Pallas. A year later, during an election campaign, Fox piled into a brawl occasioned by the factions' support for different Irish Home Rule League candidates. The Constabulary (Royal by this point) intervened in a vain attempt to settle things down — only for the fighting to continue for an hour in among, between and over the top of the constables' bayonets.

Fox Gilhooly was subsequently charged with offences (the particulars were reported in the Belfast newspaper the *Northern Whig* on the same day that the death of the explorer David Livingstone was confirmed), and on 16 July 1874 he was sentenced to five years in prison.[6]

A month later, the bishop of Cashel, the Most Reverend Dr Leahy, bemoaned that while the rest of Ireland appeared to have freed itself from the blight of faction fighting, the parishes of Pallasgrene, Kilteely and Cappamore remained 'linked with the infamy of the Three Year Old and Four Year Old factions, and with the deeds of blood done in their name'. In his Pastoral Letter he laid into the factions, characterising them as 'insane and hell-born'; describing as 'ridiculous' the long-forgotten dispute over the age of an animal; and listing the fruits of these factions as 'hatred, revenge, way-laying, maimings, breakings of skulls, bloodshed, [and] murder'.

Perhaps his words struck a chord — or perhaps the factions were simply exhausted — for on 19 August 1874 the Three Year

Olds and the Four Year Olds gathered at a small whitewashed church in New Pallas and buried the shillelagh. (It probably helped that 18 publicans decided to give up selling grog on Sundays, although they did so only after severe pressure was brought to bear by the clergy.) And Andrew left Ireland for Aotearoa.

The point of rehearsing this byzantine detail is that the son of tenant farmers, who'd been dispossessed in their own land by a colonising force, built a life for himself on the other side of the world on land taken from another people.

Andrew would have been all too familiar with the stock in trade of colonial authorities: the evictions, the confiscation of people's land, the tearing down of their houses. He was also acquainted with violence — that of the factions, but also the sort perpetrated on common people by state institutions such as the Royal Irish Constabulary. And the violence was close to home. In 1873 Andrew, his brother John and his father, Hugh, had had their own spell in jail, sentenced to a month's hard labour after being convicted of 'assault and rescue'. There is nothing in the court reports to suggest that the convictions were related to faction fighting, but Fox was certainly in the thick of things, and it seems unlikely that he was the only one of the many Gilhooly men living in and around Kilteely who wielded the shillelagh.

So it seems reasonable to suppose that Andrew's views on matters that now consume me, such as land, leases and armed constables, were coloured by the history and circumstances he was born into. Through his father's marriage into the Kennedys, who had themselves gained from the dispossession of the

Mahoneys, Andrew had already indirectly benefited from the actions of the Irish Constabulary. And he would certainly have understood what perpetual leases meant, given that they were the cause of his father Hugh's tenuous relationship with the small block of land he farmed.

For as far as I can tell (with Eddie O'Dea's considerable help), the lease for the farm that Kennedy took over from the evicted Mahoney, 28 acres of which was subsequently leased to Hugh Gilhooly, was 'at will': the agrarian equivalent of a zero hours contract. This meant that Andrew's family had no security of tenure whatsoever and could have been evicted by William Anderson, the absentee English landlord who *did* hold leases in perpetuity, at any time and without reason — as Michael Mahoney and his family had been.

My great-grandfather may or may not 'have been beset by the sins of his age'.[7] I have no way of knowing, given the absence of letters, diaries and anything else that might shed light on the kind of person he was. But Andrew must have brought all of that vulnerability and insecurity with him to this country: as Gillian has remarked about her own folk, the nature of his and his people's past was likely lodged deep in his bones. And so I can see why he might have leapt at the chance of being a landowner rather than a tenant. I can appreciate, too, that joining the AC would not have been beyond the pale.

Quite apart from the role the Irish equivalent had played in his own family's history, signing up also provided a living. The fact that he continued his military career when the AC was disbanded, rather than seeking a land grant (as was an option for men who retired), suggests that he didn't initially see service in the AC as a means to a landowning end.[8] So, yes, I can see the appeal for Andrew of breaking with his uneasy history.

Nonetheless, I can also recognise the fundamental paradox my great-grandfather's choices present. His own Irish people often suffered at the hands of the Royal Irish Constabulary; he joined the New Zealand version of that force.[9] The people of his village had had their land violently confiscated; he participated in the confiscation of the holdings of another village on the other side of the world. His father was a tenant farmer working land taken, centuries past, from his Irish ancestors; in time he would come to own land that was alienated, including through military action he had participated in, from Māori. I doubt he gave such contradictions much thought, but I still don't really know what to do with them.

More importantly, the paradox goes far deeper than the actions of individuals. One of the risks of focusing on what this or that person did or did not do is that you quickly lose sight of the fact that, whatever the actions of Ellen Foxon, Andrew Gilhooly, John Kelly or William Green, they were facilitated by institutional arrangements and forces that were far beyond their reach (and possibly their knowledge). It isn't that individuals' or families' choices do not matter, but it is the case that they are enabled — or constrained — by the legal, political, social and economic circumstances in which they are exercised. You can't sensibly keep the small stories and the big ones apart.

In Andrew's case — in the cases of all of those who migrated from there to here — empire mattered. More particularly, the laws that propelled the military and agricultural campaigns in which he participated, and which were designed to alienate Taranaki Māori from their land, were based on Irish templates. To put this another way: the small story of my great-grandfather and his wife in this country played out only because of arrangements that had been adapted from Ireland to the specifics of Aotearoa. Andrew may have thought he was leaving his homeland behind when he sailed away, but he arrived to find it here.[10]

Let me start with the New Zealand Armed Constabulary.[11] The establishment of the AC in 1867 was the result of debates that went back to 1864, when Attorney-General Henry Sewell asked of the imperial government, 'What do you mean to do when the troops are withdrawn? I will not presume at the present moment to give any definite answer to that point; but we [the colonial administration] have it in under consideration to form some sort of defence corps. It may be something on the same principle as the Irish Constabulary Force.'[12]

In the event, the Armed Constabulary Bill — the object of which was 'to raise a small police force for the purpose of securing the tranquility more especially of Native districts, on the withdrawal of the troops and the location of military settlers' — was introduced in the colonial legislature in August 1867.[13] The government had in mind something modelled on the Royal Irish Constabulary, which was 'generally acknowledged [to be] the finest force in the world.'[14]

Not all members of the legislature were convinced of the merits of this idea. Mr Burns 'hoped the House would pause before giving their sanction to this measure . . . on the ground that these Natives ought to be treated in a very different manner from shooting them down'.[15] Mr Jollie had it on good authority that 'the Irish constabulary force, although it had received high commendation, was rather defective as a police. The men were said to be above their work, and it was also said that there was too much pipeclay about them — too much adherence to the stiff formality of military discipline.' He believed '[t]hey had not been found very efficient in preventing or in detecting crime, although in respect of faction fights, riots, and that sort of thing, they had been of special service.'[16]

But the argument was to no avail, and the legislation was passed on 2 October 1867. Through a memetic process an institution created over there to pacify the Irish was copied over here and subsequently unleashed on Māori. A decade later one of those Irish people — Andrew Gilhooly — signed up to that institution, and four years after that he was standing outside Parihaka pā, ready to join an invasion.

So there is that. Now for the land. A decade after he had marched into Parihaka, and in keeping with the established imperial practice of recycling military men as civilian settlers, Andrew returned to Taranaki.[17] There were two pieces of legislation that enabled him to reinvent himself as a farmer, both passed in 1863 and both based on Irish antecedents.

The Suppression of Rebellion Act 1863 provided for the 'prompt and effectual punishment' of those engaged in 'the subversion of the authority of Her Majesty and Her Majesty's Government' (meaning those engaged in defending their own land from people trying to take it from them), and was copied, virtually word for word, from Irish legislation.[18] Indeed, Native Minister William Fox made it quite clear that '[t]he Bill which is on the table of the House has been framed strictly, and almost verbally, by reference to two Acts — one of the Irish Parliament, passed in 1799; and the other of the Imperial Parliament, in

1833. The Attorney-General has thought it desirable to adopt the phraseology of those Acts . . . as they had been concurred in by Her Majesty, and acted upon, as no doubt this Act will be similarly sanctioned.'[19]

Not everyone agreed with Fox. Henry Sewell, a former attorney-general, pointed out that the proposed law was based on legal precedent closely associated with the 'charnel house of Irish history'.[20]

As for the New Zealand Settlements Act 1863, which allowed the colonial state to take Māori land for 'public purposes', it was 'similar in title and terms to Cromwell's Act of Settlement 1652'.[21] It legitimised the confiscation of all Māori land in districts decreed to be in 'rebellion' under its companion, the Suppression of Rebellion Act (but did not stop the colonial authorities from also taking land from Māori who had *not* been in rebellion).

The Act also made the humble family farm a central instrument of colonial policy. Its preamble noted that: 'the best and most effectual means of attaining those ends ['the prevention of future insurrection or rebellion and for the establishment and maintenance of Her Majesty's authority and of Law and Order throughout the Colony'] would be by the introduction of a sufficient number of settlers able to protect themselves and to preserve the peace of the Country'.

Again dissenting voices were raised. Sir William Martin, the first chief justice of the colony, expressed his trenchant opposition in a letter to Fox, warning that the 'example of Ireland may satisfy us how little is to be effected towards the quieting of a country by the confiscation of private land; how the claim of the dispossessed owner is remembered from generation to generation, and how the brooding sense of wrong breaks out from time to time in fresh disturbance and crime'.[22] (Martin also asked that these views be forwarded to the colonial secretary, the Duke of Newcastle, who was himself worried about the likely impact of confiscation.) And one parliamentarian argued that 'it was impossible for anyone to deny that the Bill to enable the Governor to establish settlements for colonization in the Northern Island of New Zealand was inconsistent with the Treaty of Waitangi'.[23]

But neither man made any dent in the administration's plans and, two years after the passage of the New Zealand Settlements Act, some 1,275,000 acres of Taranaki land were taken from 'rebel' and non-rebel Māori alike. Eventually, 412 of those acres would become the three Gilhooly family farms.

Bluntly, then, the small story of Andrew Gilhooly cannot be separated from the big one of 'the legal, political and military processes of state forming'.[24] Neither is possible without the other; they represent a continuum, not a binary.

For a long time I thought of colonisation as something that happened out there in the realm of high politics, disconnected from the actions of people like my great-grandfather. That the big stories and the small ones had nothing to do with each other. But I've slowly come to realise they are indissolubly entwined.

John Bryce, as Gillian says, 'was doing the work of the British Empire. Making them good and great.' Joe's ancestors, William Green and his family, lived at Red House, in Takapūneke Red House Bay, where Te Tiriti o Waitangi was signed by Ngāi Tahu rangatira. Pukehinahina Gate Pā and the retribution meted out to Whakatōhea feature in John's history of Bridget and John Kelly. My ancestor participated in the invasion of Parihaka and then returned to farm confiscated land. He also had a lease on land owned by Māori, as did Jane and Tim's parents.

Ellen Foxon raises money for a church on a pā that is heartland Ngāi Tahu. The small stories and the big ones are tangled up all over the show.

Just as the decisions of colonial institutions circumscribed the scope of ordinary people's lives, so those lives contain the mundane behaviours through which colonisation was given material effect. Gillian and I agree on this: 'even though it cannot be said that they prospered', she is of the view that her Nana's family 'did serve the imperial purposes of populating the land; by sheer weight of numbers, they helped complete the work of the Colonial Office in London, the Wakefield scheme, the fraudulent laws and brute military force of various governments here'.

The two parliamentary Acts of 1863 and the legislation establishing the AC four years later laid the groundwork for the confiscation and subsequent 'settlement' of Taranaki, the Waikato and elsewhere, but the military and agricultural labour of armed constables and settler-farmers like Andrew Gilhooly was how the intent of those laws came to be inscribed on the land.

The process of inscription was literal, as the lease on the Opourapa Road farm that my great-grandfather renewed in January 1922 illustrates. '[E]very fourth year' he was required to 'paint all the outside woodwork and ironwork with two coats of proper oil-colours in a workman like manner'. He must also 'preserve and keep the premises in a clean and husbandmanlike fashion, free from all noxious weeds', and 'not plant on the premises or permit to spread thereon gorse, or furze, and will keep properly cut and trimmed all live hedges and fences'.

Should he have wished, he could 'make roads through' and 'erect or build houses or other convenient buildings' on land he farmed but which belonged to other people. He could not, however, lay claim to any 'mines, metals, minerals, coal, lignite, slate or freestone in or upon or under the land' — in the event he found any of these (he didn't) they would default to the government (not to the land's Māori owners).

This is how colonisation happened: not just in courts and legislatures but on the family farm. This is also how people got to reinvent themselves as 'settlers', the old identities left behind when they sailed away from wherever they had come into the world. Andrew's parents had leased a 29-acre piece of land from a landlord domiciled in Devon. Within two decades of leaving Ireland, he and Kate would control three farms the combined size of which was 16 times that of his parents' small Irish plot (and not very much smaller than all of the land leased out by the absentee Englishman in Kilteely parish). Those farms — circumscribed by cadastral maps which overwrote the 'indigenous cultural maps and histories' onto which they were forcibly imposed — enabled my great-grandparents to reinvent themselves as Taranaki settler-farmers.[25]

Whether they also maintained their sense of Irishness by living according to ways of knowing and being that were rooted in the places they came from I have no idea. Which is a shame, because that might have provided a way through the Irish Paradox. Had the Gilhoolys held fast to their Irishness, the atavistic memories of loss tangled up in that older way of being might well have generated a sense of identification with Māori, if not of being an interloper in someone else's country.[26]

But perhaps they simply paid Gillian's tariff, embracing their new settler identity by sloughing off all traces of the land 'where [once] we were native'. If so, it is likely they felt little or no discomfort about benefiting from Māori loss, for to be a settler was to put your past — the grinding generations of Irish poverty, the industrial wastelands, the suffocating class system — behind you, and to resolutely focus on the sunlit uplands of a bright new future in a land whose history had no claim on you.[27]

While that puzzle remains, what is perfectly clear is that the path Andrew and Kate took out of poverty was the same one down which their Irish ancestors had been marched into it: via the confiscation of people's land. In New Zealand, however, as Andrew, Kate and their descendants took the settler-colonial route, Māori were heading in the other direction, into dispossession.

6.

Digging Up
the Past

D ANISH NOVELIST STINE PILGAARD POINTS OUT
that '[W]e are all born into a story that we haven't asked
to be a part of.'[1] That may be so, but while our small
stories are not of our choosing, we do get to decide whether
we engage with the one we find ourselves in, and the degree
to which we are prepared to accept — or challenge — what we
are told.

If we take up that challenge, the process can be decidedly
uncomfortable. Sometimes what we find is not welcomed by
others. Sometimes we uncover things that we would perhaps
rather not have known. Most of Marguerite's digging has
been in Te Wai Pounamu, but she has also learned a good
deal about the colonisation of Australia, where she has lived
for many years, and where 'they didn't have militias with
the Irish,they had militias with the Aborigines. They put the
Aborigines into uniform, gave them muskets, gave them
training and then said: Go out and shoot the women and the
children and the men and take the land. And if you don't we'll
shoot you.'[2]

The work is emotional, too, each new trace of the past
packing an affective wallop commensurate with the surprise

occasioned by what has been uncovered. Realising, as Gillian does, that 'there's a whole way of life that's been built on this tawdry, dishonourable, vicious' history can take some processing — although the requisite effort pales alongside the demands that same history must make on Māori.

As I read through my great-grandfather's military service record and learned that he had been present not only for the invasion of Parihaka but also for the subsequent occupation, a sense of discomfort settled inside which has never left me. This stuff registers in the body. It might then shift to the brain or the heart or wherever — but, in the first instance, learning something that forces a fundamental re-imagination of our past is felt in the stomach.

Sometimes, too, the excavation is messy, incomplete — for even if the detail is not known, we can sense that there are bits missing. Rachel Buchanan calls this 'the presence of an absence'.[3] The blank spaces are hinted at when people express the feeling that something in their backstory is not quite right, or keep picking away at those troubling questions about how things really were. We may not know the full extent of what has been forgotten or misplaced along the way, but we know something is waiting to be found.

And sometimes digging up the past can leave us feeling unsteady on our feet, the trick of standing upright here proving more difficult than it sounds. The endless moving on, putting the past behind us and fantasising about our blameless history — perhaps this is simply what happens when the land to which we lay claim is unquiet. Perhaps, too, these unacknowledged facets of our pasts are part of the reason so many of us are constantly upping sticks, always on the prowl for a bigger house or a better piece of real estate.

We talk of this in the language of progress and of getting on in the world, but might it not also be that our constant need for movement issues from a sense of existential impermanence; from the unease that comes from knowing, deep down in the unacknowledged parts of ourselves, that we stand on shaky foundations?

❊

The work is slow, laborious, often frustrating. Neither does it really seem to end, taking on the raiment of a process of becoming rather than a state of being.

There are moments when something clangs into place, and you wonder how you could possibly have missed it before. I have long known that the Irish were unsettled by and because of the poverty created by centuries of English colonisation. I have not long known that, long after the Tudors and Cromwell, my great-grandparents — still impoverished, still landless, still dispossessed — sailed to the other side of the world where, unwittingly or otherwise, they contributed to the unsettling of mana whenua on the Taranaki coast. I do not understand why it took me so long to understand that what is an Irish staple — valorising the heroic position of the downtrodden, the oppressed, the colonised — is not extended to the tangata whenua of Aotearoa.

Six hundred years after the confiscation of land in Ireland my ancestors were *still* living in poverty, scrabbling about on small pieces of dirt owned by absentee English landlords; still bearing out Sir William Martin's warning that 'the claim of the dispossessed owner is remembered from generation to generation'. And here we are — some of us, anyway, including people with ties to Ireland who harbour strong views about perfidious Albion — telling Māori to get over it and move on.[4]

There is a double standard at work here, and the only explanation for it is that it justifies our (my) place here and conveniently absolves us (me) of responsibility for Māori disadvantage. And 'the worst of it', as Susan says, 'is that it was so recent — not 500 years ago, but the middle of the nineteenth century, a time when the British people who were directing the massacres here were well educated and knew exactly what they were doing'.

When we begin digging around in our past, familiar places — the 'tiny landscapes' that carry the memories of earlier times — start to look different.[5] Our relationship with them can start to shift, too. St Joseph's Church in New Plymouth is an important place for me. I served on its altar when I was a schoolboy (having figured out that having stuff to do — ringing bells, carrying the wine up to the priest and generally ferrying the paraphernalia of the Roman Catholic mass around the stage — was how you made it interesting); I sang alongside my great friend Bernard Leuthart in its choir; and generations of my dead — including my father — have had the Requiem Mass said for them in that church. It is part of the backdrop of my life.

I don't spend a lot of time there these days, but I like visiting it when I return to New Plymouth to see Mum. There is a quiet sense of peace to be found in sitting there, alone, thinking about how the different threads of my past come together in that place. Tucked away on the left-hand side as you enter the church is a mural by Michael Smither depicting the baptism of Christ in the river Jordan. It is one of three that Smither completed for St Joe's in the 1970s, and is saturated with his light, sharply defined edges and lush blues and greens.[6] I have looked at that mural for nearly 50 years, but rarely up close and never with much thought. Late in 2022 I went into the church with Mum to water the flowers she had prepared for that Sunday's mass. I stood in front of Smither's mural, and aspects of it I had glanced at a thousand times but never seen came into focus.

Smither's *Baptism* is taking place not in the Jordan but in Taranaki. You can tell from the shape of the rocks — they are the ones you find in the Waiwhakaiho and in the Hangatāhua. (You can also tell because Jesus is wearing stubbies and a daggy muscle shirt.) The Holy Spirit is descending in the form of a tūī, while a tuna swirls around the feet of those standing in the river. And Smither's Baptist is Māori. I can see all of it clearly now, but for half a century I saw something else entirely.

We also stir up emotions when we begin rummaging around in our history.

I'm aware of the aversion some have to engaging with these sort of issues — colonisation and the like — through the lens of feelings, and of the argument that we should instead try to understand matters dispassionately. I'm all for understanding, but am not convinced that this can take place in an affective void. I don't think it is possible (or necessarily wise) to consider our history or place in this country without engaging the emotions. 'Finding a family', as Marguerite has done, or pinning down for the first time the piece of land on which an ancestor once lived is a profoundly emotional experience, and should be acknowledged as such. Equally, it must be possible to approach these kinds of discoveries without delivering ourselves wholly into the realm of the emotional, for that way lies the abnegation of any sense of proportion.

What academics Adrienne Evans and Sarah Riley might call the 'affective texture' of the words people have sent me since writing *The Forgotten Coast* sprawls across the emotional spectrum.[7] Some carry guilt. As someone with more than a passing association with the Catholic Church I like to think I know my way around this stuff, and can distinguish between the paralysing effects of guilt and the impetus it can generate to understand what is hiding behind the historical veil.

I can also recognise when someone is trying to prevent that veil from being raised by accusing those doing the lifting of being driven by guilt. The weaponisation of guilt is one of the ways in which people who would much rather not look too closely at their past, thanks very much, denigrate the motives of those with the backbone to do so. It is a means of dismissing concerns arising from our shared history as the emotional failings of individuals, and of denying that the voices of those walking out of the historical dementia wing should be listened to. Wielding guilt in this way reveals quite a lot about the person brandishing the weapon.

But what cultural anthropologist Margaret Mead initially thought of as 'good' guilt — which, on reflection, she decided was 'a non-sensical term', so she replaced it with poet and social critic James Baldwin's suggestion, 'useful' guilt — can be the first step towards converting its immobilising effects into a productive sense of responsibility for attending to the source of the emotion.[8]

Shame, too, can be the trigger for taking responsibility for acting on aspects of our past. Marguerite's journey from the status 'not all that unsettled' to 'very unsettled' is a case in point. Early in 2022, when we first corresponded, she expressed her pride in the fact that her grandparents had 'made such significant contributions to three small communities in South Canterbury'. That view changed markedly when she learned more about the three farms her ancestors had run. 'What started as an intellectual exercise to find the farm (not knowing there were three) that I thought might have been Ngāi Tahu land,' she recalls, 'morphed into a deeply emotional journey.'

All of a sudden, 'I am faced with the dilemma: they bought the land in good faith, and were probably second owners or later after the runs were broken up. But the fact remains, they made their comfortable living out of land that was near enough to stolen: a farthing an acre, and the promised 10 per cent of land plus reserves for Ngāi Tahu was not forthcoming.' Moreover, it transpires that 'a Māori who would have been an owner of that land shears my grandfather's sheep! I mean, that sticks in my throat.'

What do you do with the dilemma that sort of knowledge creates? Marguerite's choice has been to take responsibility for acknowledging the wrong and to act on it.

At the other extreme are the words of rage, which bring to mind Ursula Le Guin's view that 'all anger is a response to fear'.[9] I don't know what it is that so frightens people who are 'sick of the maorification [sic] of everything', but my sense is that it likely has something to do with an unacknowledged dread of being forced to confront what lies behind the veil; with what happens when the ways in which we have always made sense of this country crumble and we are confronted with a very different history, the consequences of which we may need to take responsibility for understanding (if not addressing).

Perhaps, in this case, the fear is of what happens when 'beliefs that are supportive of [a] state of mind but at odds with reality' are revealed for the shabby things they are.[10]

Some of these expressions of fear and loathing in Aotearoa also make me think about writer Maria Popova's position that anger, 'nursed for its own sake, valued as an end in itself . . . fuels regression, obsession, vengeance, self-righteousness'.[11] It is pretty hard, to take one example, to say something like 'Stop beating up on the white man for a change' and come out of it looking all that good: there have certainly been victims of colonisation, but white men tend not to have been among them. As I understand it, they have often been the ones doing the beating.

But there is also a different type of anger — less obdurate, more generative — to be found in the words I've read and received. In 2019 Gloria Steinem published *The Truth Will Set You Free, But First It Will Piss You Off!* It's a great title and it captures the emotional response of a number of people who have stumbled across what actually went on here in the name of colonisation.

This kind of anger fuels a different sort of righteousness, one that sets aside the mulish insistence that colonisation was an unreservedly good thing, and instead seeks a clearer, more compassionate understanding of what it meant (and continues to mean) for Māori. One, too, that can ignite an energy harnessed and directed at the source of the anger — at the sense of intense discomfort occasioned by the knowledge of our complicity in colonisation. This is anger as a recruiting sergeant for change.

It is exemplified by Susan, an 81-year-old Pākehā, who has got a full head of steam up: 'Forgetting definitely serves those who benefit. Forgetting and denial. I'm often shocked at the overt denial I hear from Pākehā people that I get talking to. Some are outright racists but even those who consider themselves fair-minded, decent people do not accept the truth of what happened — and, more importantly, what should be done to begin to remedy what happened in the past. Witness the people nowadays who complain about Māori language beginning to be used on radio and elsewhere. Or the outrage at the Three Waters proposal. Or people who say Māori get too many advantages. It's completely repulsive. What really bothers me is to know that so many "ordinary" people vote for those who are racist. Don't they care? Clearly not.'

I think about what lies behind all of this emotion, and wonder if part of it might be that many Pākehā are 'fretful sleepers', children of colonisation who wish to be left to live in a 'wishfully untroubled world'.[12] But of course the place in which we live is far from untroubled, and the anxiety seeps through in all sorts of ways.[13]

I'm interested in this, in how we react when our sleep is disturbed. For some — including those whose stories are in this book — there is a pull, a need to apprehend both the nature of our historical foundations and how to live well on them. But those who've sent me abusive messages, and many of those opposing the Ōtorohanga College students' petition, have resorted to anger, unsettled, perhaps, by what lies just beneath the surface.

Susan is right. There is a sort of cultural thinness on display here; a defensiveness, as if some flaw in the rough scribble of our stories has been exposed, producing an aggressive determination not to engage with — or even to countenance the possibility of — other ways of thinking about our histories.

You could call this 'settler fragility', as Avril Bell does — the 'defensive, emotional responses that white people have when confronted with discussions of racism' and which 'work to maintain the (racist) status quo by shutting down the conversation and turning attention to the hurt feelings of the ("beleaguered") white person'.[14] Or you might think of it as an instance of what the American philosopher Charles Mills calls 'non-knowing', a kind of ignorance based on a continuous process of misrepresentation, evasion and self-deception, at the end of which it becomes impossible even to accept the possibility of an alternative understanding. A 'non-knower' does not refuse to concede that a different point of view may exist; rather, any such perspective has become inaccessible. It is — quite literally — not knowable.[15]

Perhaps the anger is a reaction to the threat some see to what they imagine this nation to be. Democratic theorist Benedict Anderson speaks of the nation (any nation, but let's talk about ours) as an imagined community.[16] Anderson would say that New Zealand is imagined in the sense that we make it up with our symbols (beaches, baches, anything Anzac) and our rituals (being sweet as and all good, trying hard to not stand out, punching above our weight), and also in the way we identify — through the constant evocation of our symbols and performance of our rituals — as part of this community. He doesn't mean that New Zealand is ephemeral or insubstantial: he simply means that it is as much a state of mind and a collection of practices as it is a place.

I don't know what sort of image exists in the minds of those who object to a polite exchange about colonisation. Perhaps this

New Zealand would once again have exemplary race relations if only stroppy Māori and guilt-ridden Pākehā would stop talking about Pukehinahina Gate Pā, Parihaka and confiscated land and just go away. And stop holding their damn 'slivers of mirror' up to the 'ordinary and the everyday' and making everyone feel uncomfortable.[17] Whatever that imagined place is, when its foundations are questioned — and a different imaginary community is proposed — some people don't react well.

(The imagining of New Zealand in ways that gloss over the unpleasant bits has been going on for a long time. In 1867 Sir George Grey addressed a crowd in Tīmaru, and suggested that 'this colony is what may be called a colony without blame. Our greatest enemies cannot say that anyone ever came here either to destroy the native race or to seize their land.'[18] This was just three years after Rangiaowhia and two since virtually the entirety of Taranaki had been confiscated by the Crown. But Grey had clearly convinced himself that it was all good — because if the land was empty, surely we needn't feel bad about taking it?)

Or perhaps something altogether more elemental and far more unsettling is going on. 'In ancient Scotland,' I learn from Gillian, 'the sluagh were the damaged souls of the dead who had not been laid to rest, and they roamed the land, seeking out those amongst the living who were susceptible, who had no firm ground of their own. The sluagh could visit upon these people their own broken souls.' Gillian has heard the voices of the sluagh in this country many times over the years. She heard them 'when Dame Naida Glavish said kia ora', and 'again after Judy Bailey said pō marie, peaceful evening, on the television news, and once more after Dame Hinewehi Mohi sang the national anthem in te reo'. She sees the sluagh, too, in the early settler-colonisers' greed for other people's land. Sees in this the behaviour of 'broken-souled people' estranged from the numinous and torn from the clan. People who were — and whose descendants perhaps still are — fretful sleepers.

I think about Gillian's words in the context of some of the language used in the stories we tell about our pioneering pasts. At the heart of these accounts there is a rupture between the land and those who walk it. We talk of breaking in the land, clearing the bush and controlling the gorse — as if the land is the adversary that needs to be subdued lest it rise up against us. As if it recognises us for what we were (and perhaps still are): interlopers who sundered the land's ties with the first people. But what those 'short, small, heavy words' of domination — cut, chop, slash, burn — obscure is everything that was here before the survey pegs, the fence line and the boundary markers; before we erased the bush and burned 'the very surface of the earth'.[19]

Deep histories of the land. Stories of those displaced from their whenua. Other lives lived before we arrived, and which were fractured so that we might become these new things, New Zealanders. We use this blunt, bludgeoning language without thinking much about it, but when we do we are not only invoking an imaginary New Zealand but we are also — carelessly or by design — obliterating an earlier Aotearoa.

This, too, is a form of violence, and I suspect most of us don't give all that much thought to the material impacts it has had. But Kiaran does. 'Speaking to my grandfather,' he reflects, 'I think they saw purchasing land from the government which

$A 108

MEMORIAL SCHEDULE

NAME OF BLOCK: WAIOTAMA 6B 2B (Egmont c.c) AREA: 15acs 0r 30.5p

b. 14.78hq

N.B. — The order or title notice should be referred to for search purposes.

Nature of Order or Instrument	Date	Checked	Reference
L.T. Title: C.T 14/107Pt			
Alienation File: 3/6247			
Alienations: Lease over 6B2 expired 1/4/65.			
Liens: Survey: None recorded.			
Subject to:-			
Rates: Secured by C/Os as under:-			
C/O 256 - 1/4/25-31/3/38 £11-19-10			
plus costs 10/-			
C/O 582 - 1/4/28-31/3/30 £8-19-1 plus			
costs 8/-.			
All in favor of Egmont County.			
A release of these orders is held in			
the L.T. Office unregistered.			
Not yet Surveyed: Copy of sketch plan attached.			
Copies of minutes refer to Waiotama 6B 2A			
Entered in European Register 9.1.68			
Europeanisation Deferred. Survey Required.			2.7.68.

Prepared by:

had been confiscated was just the natural order of things. There was (is) a line of thinking that "the Maoris weren't using the land in any productive way so we might as well have it". Ironic that so many Irish were driven from their land but they felt OK about taking it, albeit indirectly, from Māori.'

Kiaran has identified the two most powerful logics that people deploy to justify the historic alienation of Māori land. First (putting aside the small matter of determining what 'productive' looks like), isn't there some natural, immutable requirement to put land to productive use? And second, if the land has already been taken by the state, you are not actually doing the taking when you buy the farm. What you're doing is making the most of an opportunity, which is an altogether different thing. The mouths of gift horses and so forth.

Here are a couple of examples of what this sort of thinking can lead to in the real world. In the interests of opening up 'non-productive' land owned by Māori for (productive) settlement, the Native Land Settlement Act 1907 entitled Maori Land Boards to compulsorily vest 'unutilised' Māori land in themselves, and to require Māori landowners to sell half the vested land.[20] Forced sales, in effect, that left even less land for the mokopuna.

The view that land must be productive — that this is somehow the natural way and that people who haven't got that memo deserve to lose their land — hasn't gone away. Neither has governments' appetite to impose it on Māori. In 2013, the panel reviewing Te Ture Whenua Māori Act 1993 'proposed significant changes to the administration of Māori land, including a diminished role for the Māori Land Court, new categories of owners ("engaged" versus "disengaged"), [and] the provision to appoint external managers for land owned by "disengaged" or absent owners'.[21] These days there are plenty of Pākehā who chafe at government intervention; can you imagine their response if they had to endure this kind of intrusion?

If words can be used to suppress so, too, can their absence. The novelist and memoirist Charlotte Grimshaw has spoken of 'the destructive effect of silence'.[22] She talks of things that took place within a family that was all 'front and face'.[23] I think this also describes the general disposition of the cheerleaders of the orthodox settler-pioneer story, which is all about the presentation of a particular story of thrusting progress, who fail to examine (much less acknowledge) that there must also be a 'back and behind', a deeper story, one kept in the shade and out of view.

Grimshaw has her parents' generation in her sights when she writes, 'If anything went wrong, they had to suppress it, move on, pretend it didn't happen — and go on messing things up'.[24] But she may as well be talking about battalions of Pākehā storytellers, each one of us who cleaves to histories that laud our pioneer forebears but which effortlessly erase, ignore or smooth over the distasteful stuff.

It's as if we want a library with just one book on the shelf. If telling your own (true) story — and having it heard — is existentially critical, as Grimshaw insists is the case, what are we doing to Māori when we refuse to listen to their accounts, or to accept that theirs might depart from our Pākehā story in some fundamental ways?

7.

Beneficiaries
of Injustice[1]

U SUALLY WE THINK OF TIME AS A RESOURCE that we have too much or, more often, too little of. We might also treat it as a horizon towards or away from which we are moving. The standard position on the view receding into the distance behind us is that the past is . . . well, you know, it's the past. It happened; it's done and dusted. We're moving on. Flick back to the views of those who expressed their displeasure with Ōtorohanga College students Waimarama Anderson and Leah Bell and you will see this position on full display.

Virtually all of those submissions reflected a belief that the effects of events that once happened on that far horizon are restricted to and stay in that place. There is no path from there to here — indeed, there cannot be, for to countenance this possibility is to accept that when we reach the temporal shore towards which we are travelling there will be a reckoning.

Look closer, though, and things are not so straightforward. People who want the past to behave properly and stay where it belongs often assert that certain aspects of it are incontrovertible truths (that colonisation was good for Māori; that Māori were a backward people before the British saved them from their barbarism), and use those imagined truths to justify views held in the present (that we should all stop harping on about colonisation; that Māori should be grateful they were colonised by the British rather than the French). In such cases there *is* a path between past and present and it is daily trod. It just isn't acknowledged.

Historian Charlotte Macdonald is good on this stuff, taking issue with the 'common sense, but mistaken, notion that the past is sequestered in and by time . . . that historical events exist behind a closed door, sealed off from the present [and] thus "dead": actions and speech acts with no pulse, drained of any capacity to affect the present.'[2] What she is doing, of course, is inviting us to consider that the door of history might, in fact, be wide open, enabling a steady flow of traffic in both directions: the acts of the dead resonating in the lives of the living, and those in the present seeking to understand the consequences for their own lives of actions taken long ago.

Keith Ovenden observes that 'history — both the sort that is written down and the sort that is not — not only shapes and binds us, but also betrays and exhausts us'.[3] He, too, is saying that we are a consequence of our pasts: they are always with us. We can turn away from that darkening shore, but it will never vanish over the horizon.

Many of those I listened to while pulling this book together are frequent travellers through Macdonald's door, trying to figure out the shape and flavour of things from the past from which they benefit today. They do not buy the 'bad history/ good present' schtick that allows us to pass moral judgment on the actions of dead colonisers (John Bryce is always a favourite) but avoid questioning how what occurred then might shape our own lives now.[4]

Privilege is a word I struggle with, not least because I'm conscious that I get to enjoy quite a lot of it and that from time to time I may get a little sanctimonious when this is pointed out to me. I'm male (so I generally don't need to worry if my drink has been spiked or if I need to cross the road to remain safe), an academic (so not too many worries on the income front) and Pākehā (which we'll get to shortly). I am also wary because the language of privilege is liable to go down poorly — and with good reason — among people who have little or nothing in the way of wealth or income; the kind of whom the writer Owen Marshall might have said, 'He's slogged, though, you have to give him that.'[5]

I prefer the term structural advantage, which we used as sociology students in the 1980s to explain the benefits baked into the institutions within which we live our lives but which are available only to those who get to write the relevant rules of the game. The rules, of course, are rarely visible to the players. They are assumed to be the normal state of affairs — just the way things are — and therefore not so much unremarkable as invisible. And all the more potent for being so. But 'structural advantage' has four more syllables than 'privilege', and little going for it in terms of emotional impact. Plus, 'Pākehā structural advantage' lacks the alliterative thump of 'Pākehā privilege'. It's clunky, overly sincere. So, privilege it will have to be.

In the sense that I'm using it here, 'privilege' refers to an advantage that flows from a preferred status (a particular ethnicity, say, or gender), and that works to the benefit of those who have it and to the exclusion or detriment of those who don't.[6] It is not something we earn through our own efforts, and we may not even be aware we gain from this particular type of 'breeze at [our] back'.[7] Plenty of people, however, understand the word to refer specifically to material advantage: assets, a nice car, a bach up in Taupō or down in Queenstown.

So it's easy to see how wires can get crossed, and why some Pākehā struggling to get by get pissed off when it is suggested that they are privileged. If the politics of socio-economic class are more salient for you than those of ethnicity, phrases like 'Pākehā privilege' (much less 'white supremacy') might well be a wee bit triggering.

It isn't helpful, either, or accurate, to assume that everyone with family who once owned land (or still does) spends their down time lounging around at the bach. Jane and Tim's dad left school 'when he was 14 and he had to milk cows night and morning from the age of eight. To me,' Tim wrote, 'while it is possible that the land at Pihama was acquired on the basis of less than fair means, I do not feel that this has flowed through as significant privilege in my particular family.'

Both sides of Win's family also owned land at various times, but 'a combination of early deaths, failed businesses, the Depression and large families was the reason none of this passed down' to her. And Andrew and Kate Gilhooly ran three small farms, but by the time the value contained in those properties filtered down to Mum's generation, the extent of the direct monetary benefit was the £100 she and most of her sisters received in her father's will (the boys got a bit more, as did Cath, because she was a nun).

All the same, the land supported the family in other ways. This is why we have to reckon with the notion of privilege, and to disentangle it from notions of wealth, because the benefits it bestows are not necessarily material and not always immediately obvious to those who enjoy them. Here are some of the ways in which Pākehā privilege applies to me.

It means I can drive along the South Road and see a landscape (great views of the mountain today), rather than the traumascape which those whose whānau had land taken from them are likely to see and in which 'the past is never quite over'.[8] In doing so I bear out author and academic Robert Macfarlane's observation that '[w]hen we look at a landscape we do not see what is there, but largely what we think is there. In other words, we interpret [landscape] in the light of our own experiences and memory, and that of our shared cultural memory.'[9] I see farms that gave my family a start here; mana whenua might see land that was taken forcibly from them and never returned.

It means that for decades I got to walk past the photo of Andrew Gilhooly lined up alongside his AC mates at the Rāhotu Domain in 1881 and not really see it, much less engage with what it so obviously meant. It means I did not even have to worry about any of this history until I stumbled over it in my mid-fifties. It also means that, had I wished, I could have continued to avoid the 'unhomely stories about home', and remained blithely ignorant of the intersection of the big story of colonisation with my family's small story.[10]

Moreover, when I feel a little overwhelmed by all this Pākehā privilege stuff, I can put my writing away and pick up something less demanding — the latest Booker winner, perhaps, or a nice flat white. Perhaps I'll come back to the privilege thing a bit later on but, you know, whatever — only if I feel like it. These are all choices denied to the descendants of Taranaki Māori.

Of course I'm not the only one to have become aware of the existential privilege of not having to know certain things (much less live with their consequences) unless I choose to, of being 'able to live here as if Māori don't exist'.[11] Shortly after arriving in Aotearoa from Canada in the early 1970s, Susan enrolled in a Māori language course at the University of Auckland and began reading up on New Zealand history. And as can happen when we start paying attention, things began to come into focus; Susan recalls 'starting to realise the true story of theft and massacre'.

She understands that 'it was a similar story in the US and Canada with First Nations people' but also knows that 'as a young person growing up in Canada I had no idea of the atrocities that were happening. Even during my years at McGill University, studying sociology among other subjects, it was never mentioned. I now know that children were being taken from their families at the very time I was trotting off to my lectures. How did I not know this?'

Her question might (once) have been rhetorical, but it is one that many of us are now seeking answers to. There are all sorts of reasons why Susan didn't know what was going on as she trundled off to her classes, and some of them had to do with what she did — and more importantly, did not do — while she was in them. I can't say with certainty who or what she read in her courses, but I suspect I'm on solid ground in assuming that she cut her sociological teeth on a canonical diet of Marx, Durkheim and Weber (maybe Talcott Parsons), and did not come across a single Indigenous scholar.

So, some forms of knowledge will have been considered legitimate and others dismissed as arcane (or as superstition rather than knowledge), and certain authors will have been recognised as 'knowing agents' while others would have been ignored. That is one of the reasons why Susan didn't know.

Debbie Broughton (of Taranaki Iwi, Te Aitanga-a-Hauiti, Ngāti Porou and Ngāpuhi) expresses this point far better than I can in one of her poems: '[W]hich reminds me of that legislation lecture | about how Pākehā law | is *the* law | blah blah parliamentary sovereignty | blah blah rule of law | and then he asked if there was any other source of law | coz now we have the burden of proving him wrong?' You get her point.[12]

It can be subtle, this stuff, and insidious, the benefits sometimes not apparent until much later on in life — and even then, only if we're prepared to look for and acknowledge them, rather than chalk everything up to our own efforts. 'There were times when this became a material advantage,' says Gillian of her grandparents, 'for they knew their way around the social and political structures, and even the youngest sons could get a start in life on other farms. My father, for example, was settled on what was then known as marginal land, and was in fact venerated but confiscated land, near Te Hoe-o-Tainui, the resting-place of the paddle of the Tainui waka. Later, an old family friend stepped in to help prevent financial disaster in our part of the family, securing an arrangement with a gentlemen's handshake that was honoured by both sides. We are still reaping the benefits of that.'

In response to a question about how her ancestors' circumstances have contributed to her own situation, Jane gets straight to the point: 'Of course I have profited from the actions of previous generations,' she says, 'and the key aspect is that my family, at every generation until the 1970s, farmed cheap land and, especially post WW2, reaped the rewards. This meant that, unlike previous generations who left school as soon as was legal, my cousins and I all stayed to Year 13 (Form 7) and most of us undertook tertiary training. Our forebears had aspirations and it was expected that if we could afford to do so we would fulfil those aspirations. We *could* afford to do so. Our Māori school friends could not.'

Aidan is pretty frank about this, too. 'I am fortunate to have a connection to Taranaki through my ancestors having owned, farmed, and/or held property there,' he says. 'I have benefited from university educated parents and their subsequent job security. At some stage I will benefit from inherited wealth built on the lands that were once confiscated.'

Justine takes matters a little further, reflecting on the 'more intangible benefits' that comprise part of her inheritance, 'such as growing up in a country where my Pākehā culture was dominant and valued. My immediate family always had a warm, dry house to live in (eventually one that we owned), healthy and plentiful food, my parents were comfortably off, education within the Pākehā system was valued and encouraged and I never had to worry about racism or discrimination. I don't think we can underestimate the effect of being part of the dominant culture, with our presence in Aotearoa validated by a widespread (if fragile) narrative that our forebears helped to "build the nation".'

The benefit of belonging to the group that gets to write the rules and draw the maps comes up time and again in my conversations with the unsettled. 'Crudely expressed,' says Gillian, 'we inherited white skin, too. Though we grew up in the old way, we could still pass as people belonging to the world based on the Western nuclear family; we did not have to endure the prejudices and cruelties inflicted upon those whose skin was coloured differently.'

Someone else writes that 'in some subtle way I think that being Pākehā and from a relatively wealthy farming family gave me some advantages over other Kiwis. Education was valued by my family and higher learning encouraged. It was only later in life that I came to realise that such basic things were not universal. So, I recognise now that despite the trauma of my parents' dysfunctional marriage, there were still a few scraps of privilege remaining. Examples would be my mother passing on her love of reading, there were books on the shelves, art on the walls and records with the stereo. Māori who were dispossessed of their lands and livelihood had a far greater trauma to deal with.'

As Pākehā, it isn't hard to avoid thinking about these inbuilt advantages. If we are of a mind to do so, and plenty of us are, it is fairly straightforward to convince ourselves that colonisation is the business of governments and their departments, parliaments, courts and armies. Easy, too, to dismiss it as something that happened once upon a time and to other people. Easier still 'to assign [our] fortune to merit and others' disadvantage to personal blame, bad luck, or lack of hard work rather than acknowledging and understanding structural forces'.[13]

Those informal rules of the game which shape the way we live together — things we take for granted and think are natural, normal, universal and timeless — work to some people's advantage but make others' lives more challenging. Susan puts us all straight on the matter: 'Also, it is a known fact that those who succeed almost always attribute their success to their own efforts,' she states firmly, '[s]o they do not look back and understand that they would not be where they are today unless predecessors had made it possible for them and in New Zealand that means taking things from Māori. Those acts disappear from their memories.'

Kiaran backs her up: 'Land, money, education: all these things were made possible by the confiscation,' he muses. 'When Honora died in 1940 she (or the trust) owned by my count six farms, along with a very favourable lease on Māori land on the Skeet Road. I don't know what occupation Honora had but I suspect she was a servant. So, from an 18-year-old servant to matriarch with half a dozen farms! That kind of good luck makes me very suspicious.'

Much the same thing happened to my great-grandparents. Andrew was born on a 29-acre farm that his father leased from an Englishman. By 1902 he controlled 314 acres; add Kate's farm, and the two of them held sway over 412 acres. Andrew's people had been tenant farmers for generations: within just 26 years he had sorted that out. There is no earthly way he could have managed this in Ireland. There is no earthly way he could have managed it here, either, had it not been for the availability of cheap land that had been taken from Māori.

Susan, Justine, Kiaran and I are not saying that people didn't work hard. We are simply suggesting that, in the cases of our families, it is not possible — unless we are prepared to indulge in weapons-grade self-delusion — to explain the magnitude of the economic, social and cultural transformations that took place in some families within a single generation or two solely by reference to individual merit, hard yakka and the grace of our God.

And this raises a question, at least for me, about the material foundations of our ideas about social mobility. The notion that this is a country in which you can haul yourself up by dint of individual endeavour is a powerful one, but it has its historical roots in the experiences of people like my great-grandparents. Who did indeed reinvent themselves — on the basis of confiscated land.

The fact that the land had already been taken by the time they purchased or leased their farms is beside the point. However decent, hardworking and God-fearing they may have been, this is not about individuals' merits: this is about a colonial system that benefited some at the expense of others.

There are people who will violently disagree with this kind of thinking. But it is impossible to evade the matter when we figure out that our own family history contains the calling cards of colonisation: invasions, occupations, benefiting from the theft of others' land. When we see our own history reflected in these events, colonisation abruptly stops being abstract and becomes immediate.

John may be speaking for a growing number of us when he says that, having done serious legwork on Bridget and James Kelly's pasts, he 'can't ignore the fact that they were involved in one of the more blatant pieces of looting of Māori land and property that occurred in New Zealand'.

When those sorts of scales drop from our eyes, colonisation plummets from the realm of high politics into that of the personal and the everyday — and the issue of privilege cannot be avoided. The coffee goes cold, the Booker turns out to be a dud, and out of the corner of my eye I see Debbie Broughton's razor-sharp poetry ('Decolonisation | is your job | not mine | I'm working on | the re-Taranaki-fication | of Te Aro Pā') propped up against Rachel Buchanan's stunning *Te Motunui Epa*.[14] So it's back to the privilege thing.

＊

The three Gilhooly farms are where, for me, colonisation and Pākehā privilege cease being nebulous concepts and take material form. I can't precisely calculate the extent of the economic benefit that my great-grandparents gained from that land, because their wills do not specify the full value of the assets that were placed in trust following their deaths and there are few extant farm records to speak of. But I do have five small portraits of how my family has profited from the 'historical windfall' that came its way on the basis of land confiscated from Taranaki Māori.[15]

First: the combined purchase price of sections 44 and Parihaka A came to $329,698 (in today's currency), none of which went to the iwi whose land they were.[16] Just under $70,000 went to the state for the South Road farm, and the balance went to Hori Teira, from whom Kate Gilhooly purchased Parihaka A. Actually, it's not even clear that Teira — who had been charged an occupation licence to live on his own land before selling it to Kate — ever received that money.

The Native Land Act 1909 gave the District Maori Land Boards the legal right to hold onto proceeds from the sale of land 'if [they] thought that the owner was not "capable" of controlling the money'.[17] The paper trail that sits behind the Waitangi Tribunal's 1996 Taranaki Report suggests that this is precisely what happened to Teira when he sold Parihaka A to my great-grandmother. If that is so, then Māori got none of the money from the purchase of those farms. At. All.

The second snapshot concerns the lease taken out on the Opourapa Road farm in 1902. I don't know how much of the rent made its way to the farm's Māori owners, nor how many there were, because the lease makes no mention of them. But what is clear is that the rent my great-grandfather paid remained fixed at £35 per annum (payable in twice-yearly instalments) for 21 years, and that when it was renewed in 1922 for a further two decades the Public Trustee bumped it up to £47. Across a 44-year period the rent paid on Section 2 Block 13 of the Cape Survey District increased by just £12. That does not look like a great rate of return to me. There is no record of what the Māori owners might have had to say on the matter.

Then there are the contents of the will left by Richard Gilhooly, the fourth of my great-grandparents' six children. On his death in 1955, Dick, who was a Roman Catholic priest, left the equivalent of $1353 to the Church so that 25 masses could be said for the repose of his soul, a further $27,027 to the Wellington Archdiocese's Seminary Fund, and close to $200,000 to his sisters Liz and Moll. Priests do not draw large salaries (and Dick, who died at the age of 44, spent nearly all of his working life incapacitated by tuberculosis), so I assume that in the main these figures represent his share of the family's accumulated wealth.[18]

The fourth and fifth sketches come courtesy of the 1953 statements from the trustees of the respective estates of Andrew and Kate Gilhooly. (He had been dead for 30 years, she for just 12 months.) There was a lot going on. Money was coming into Andrew's estate from the Cape Egmont and Rāhotu dairy companies, the local abattoir, stock agents and some bloke called Vercoe who owed rent. It was going out to the fertiliser company, to 'J. Maxwell for the provision of manures' and to the Māori Trustee (for the Opourapa Road farm, presumably).[19]

Kate's estate was still shaking down. There was much buying and selling of lambs, ewes and cows; there were toll fees to be paid; in New Plymouth Foley's Fabrics was owed a small amount, as were Remington the grocers and the Farmers Co-op; and there was rent due to the Aotea Land Board (for what, I've no idea). Work your way through the evidence of a busy local community to the bottom lines, and you'll find that Andrew's estate was in credit to the tune of $915,667 while Kate's had a credit balance of $325,576.

Small-scale farmers like my ancestors were not the kinds of people to leave their fingerprints all over the historical record, and these five vignettes are all I've been able to uncover of the goings-on of the three family farms. But they are a sufficient basis on which to venture two observations. The first is that the land provided an economic foundation from which my great-grandparents and their descendants would go on to buy other properties, establish businesses, gain educations, support the endeavours of children, bequeath money to their own descendants and so on. It got them all started.

What's more, there is a multiplier effect at work here, each new generation benefiting from the affordances handed down by the one above and producing its own. We like to think we've earned what we have, but there's a reason why the intergenerational transfer of wealth is 'the most significant factor in the current socio-economic position of descendants'.[20]

The whare raupō in which Kate Fleming's brothers first lived became huts and then houses; money earned from the farms was invested, returns improved and more land purchased; children were sent off to school and the family's financial wherewithal transformed into other forms of capital; one thing led to another and people moved on and up in the world. But the land is at the beginning of it all.

Again, to labour a point, I'm not suggesting that people didn't and haven't worked hard, simply that inheritance really helps — and that there is no getting away from the fact that the passing on of resources down through the years is one of the reasons my life (and others') has played out as it has. Not just economic resources, either, but the other types of capital — social, emotional, educational — that flow from economic security. This is what economic privilege looks like. And you don't earn it — you're born into it.

What is more, it is not something that belongs in the past. Those farms passed out of Gilhooly hands long ago, but they are still giving. The opportunity they provided my great-grandparents to establish themselves here in Aotearoa has been renewed with each subsequent generation.

But the giving is to me and my relations, not to those from whom the land was taken. The snapshots I've provided here represent a fragment of what has been denied the people who had lived on sections 44 and 102 of Block 12 Cape Survey District, and on Parihaka A, for centuries before my lot arrived. Scale that up. Those three farms constituted the tiniest fleck — just 0.03 per cent — of the 1,275,000 acres taken from mana whenua in Taranaki in 1865.

It is not for me to say whether material considerations are the most consequential of the losses wrought by colonisation on Taranaki Māori, but they are certainly not insignificant. And what has been taken is not simply the asking price of a couple of small dairy farms but all of the value, tangible and intangible, that subsequently flowed from that land down the long years that followed its purchase by my great-grandparents — and all that is yet to flow in those which lie ahead.

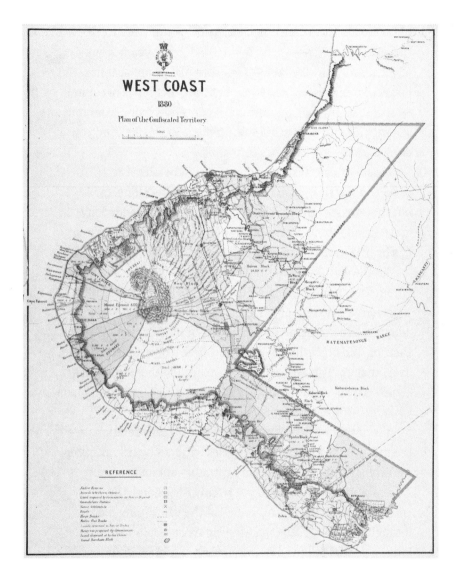

All of the land to the west of the confiscation line — everything in what Rachel Buchanan has called the 'great knuckle of Taranaki' — was taken by executive fiat in the mid-1860s. Most of it was subsequently sold by the colonial state to Pākehā settler-farmers like my great-grandparents. *Puke Ariki, ARC2004-325*

Once we start thinking about it we start seeing the dividends of colonisation everywhere, including in places we might not ordinarily look (unless we happen to be a descendant of those upon whom it was visited). This from Rachel Buchanan:

> The owners of blocks both north and south of Parihaka were charged for surveying, fencing, draining and road building costs. Roads were the most expensive. My ancestors had to pay for the roads that were built through land that they would never be able to farm ... Māori owners received minimal rents from their tenants and Reserves Trustee Wilfred Rennell admitted that rents were particularly low in Ōpunake, especially once money for roads and surveys had been deducted ... Meanwhile settlers claimed their rents were too high and many either refused to pay or negotiated significant reductions.[21]

Drains, roads, surveyed farms, fence lines. In the case of Māori leasehold land, the fruits of that agricultural infrastructure are enjoyed by Pākehā settler-farmers and their descendants but substantially paid for by Māori who could neither live on nor work their own land. (As it happens, this was not all that Māori landowners paid for. They were also charged 'survey fees, Crown and Native Land rates, costs for bush-felling, the 7.5% commission that the Public Trustee charged, land tax, interest on the overdrafts, and the cost of advertising the leases'.)[22] And all that rent not paid: more benefits that accrued to Pākehā at the expense of Māori.

To reiterate: the political economy of injustice didn't deliver simply a one-off economic jolt. The benefits were cumulative, as the roads paid for by Māori carried the milk to the new dairy factories to be churned into butter and made into cheese. As rents withheld were invested in improvements to the farms that generated profits, which were ploughed back into the land out of which Māori had been locked. An endless, virtuous cycle of accumulation, Adam Smith's hand not even hidden. Over the years it adds up. As do the losses sustained and the opportunities forgone by Māori.

The material stuff is important, of course, but Pākehā privilege takes many forms, some of which have nothing to do with economic wealth. Chief amongst these is the sense of place that stems from long generations of a family's presence in and on this land. Susan, for one, is conscious of 'a sense of having a right to be here, and when I go anywhere, I have no fear that I will be unwelcome because of the colour of my skin, or a moko, or anything like that. I will go unremarked. I often think about that, when I go somewhere among a group who don't know me at all. I think: What if I were Māori — how would I be received?'

For Jane, what has been handed down is a 'strong sense of belonging to Aotearoa New Zealand, and Taranaki in particular. I have no land to stand on, but I do identify with the Coast. When I drive north from Wellington I look across the bight to see if Taranaki maunga is standing up out of the sea and I feel a thrill if the air is clear enough to afford a sighting.' Tim, too, feels 'a belonging to the coast of Taranaki, even though I have not lived there since I was 12'.

A woman who emailed me from Wellington reflected that she has 'an identity handed down to me that I have questioned and reshaped over decades. That my ancestors came here early on in the colonisation process generates a sense of being invested in the people and the land that make up this country. The values of social justice that I have both inherited and chosen also provide me a "place to stand". It has taken considerable personal work to do the "facing in" that I believe is needed to begin to reconcile the past and present, and this is ongoing.'

Joe has also 'inherited a strong sense of place — a sense of having licence to stand in this country. A sense of belonging.' For him, as for others who have thought on this long and hard, the sense of attachment is not acquisitive or proprietorial; not some fragile object needing to be locked away from others. The inheritance may be born out of all that the colonisation of this country has been and remains, but it has become generative, producing an ethic of responsibility and just action. Joe knows that 'lighting the flame for another does not mean my own goes out'.

I have some idea of what these people are talking about. Andrew Gilhooly and Kate Fleming were born into Irish poverty. In the space of a generation they would cast off that yoke and recreate themselves as respected members of the coastal Taranaki settler community. Find security after centuries of vulnerability, find solid ground on which they could stand. Theirs. To be a settler is to shed old identities and acquire new ones which quickly become 'natural' as they are passed down to others for whom they are all that has ever been known.

The Taranaki coast that exists in my imagination is like this. It forms a significant part of my cultural inheritance, and a major chunk of my sense of who I am and where I come from. It provides me with emotional, temporal and cognitive coordinates: I can find my way back there in several different ways. It is not some abstract thing that can be sneeringly dismissed as 'identity politics', and is no less (indeed, much more) valuable than whatever fractional material gain might have come to me down the years from those three Gilhooly farms. But given its origins, this identity claim is fraught — just ask those on whose land it rests.

Belatedly, too, I have come to realise that these ties to particular places endure across time and space. They are mobile, capable of travel, and tend to follow us around even if we no longer have a personal connection with the land on which our forebears established themselves. What's more, the places in which those roots were put down continue to call.

And so Marguerite says that she wants 'to go and see that land. I want to look at it. I want to look at it because I have family who once lived there and farmed on it, but I want to look at it through different eyes and say: "You know, this land was in my family but it really never should have been." Or it shouldn't have been under the circumstances in which it came to be.'

Marguerite brings us to a central dilemma. How do we stand on land which has been harnessed to our own stories when we know the circumstances in which that came to be? The question applies not only to those of us with pasts, presents or futures that rest on land acquired through dubious or violent means. I suspect there are Pākehā who think it does (which is another way of dodging the issue), but my sense is that whether farming on confiscated land in the Waikato or renting an apartment in downtown Ōtautahi Christchurch, the challenge lingers: how do we both open ourselves to the imprint of colonisation and figure out our bearings in this place we now call home? We don't get to avoid that by pointing to the layers of time, governing institutions, property ownership and concrete that insulate us from the whenua. Here, we are all beneficiaries of injustice.

Beyond writing this quandary out in so many words, it's difficult to know what to do with it. One approach I've tried is essentially one of denial. Not, I hasten to add, in the sense the term is used to repudiate facts that are demonstrably true (US presidential election results; the efficacy of vaccines; that sort of thing). Rather, the idea is to renounce things I have long taken for granted or assumed were mine as of right: the right to knowledge of all subjects, say, or to exercise my voice simply because I have an opinion. That sort of thing.

I am still learning the ins and outs of the methodology of renunciation. I am no adept, but am slowly understanding what it means to make room for others by stepping back and taking up a position on the fringes. I am getting the hang of talking less and listening more. I am figuring out how to deny myself things rather than claim them, and to balance the vocabulary of rights with that of responsibilities.

All of this goes against my natural disposition. I have been raised to be inquisitive; it is the basis of my day job. Generally this is an asset, but it can manifest as acquisitive entitlement: 'Look, there's a bright, shiny new piece of knowledge — I'll have that, thanks very much.' I am slowly realising that there are some things that are simply not mine to know. That there are times when my desire to learn and the object of my curiosity should be kept apart, and I need to pull my head in.

When we get this process of decoupling right, what some- times results is a sort of nothingness in which, nonetheless, potential exists. Space in which to see the object rather than the category. Time between stimulus and response. Silence that allows old certainties or troublesome dilemmas to be contemplated differently.

Here are two matters I have been thinking about while in those liminal places. First, I have been wondering about the ethics of using 'tūrangawaewae' to describe where I come from. That word encompasses horizons of time and ties to land whose scope and depth I do not fully comprehend, although I'm pretty sure it all amounts to a bit more than simply having lived in a place for several generations and, as Gillian puts it, 'having a nice feeling about it or wanting to do right by it or whatever'.

Given the particulars of my own small story, I cannot in good conscience invoke 'tūrangawaewae' when I speak of the places in this country which are important to me. To do so would mean making a claim to land that was once the tūrangawaewae of other people but is no longer — their tie severed to enable mine. Other Pākehā do use the term, and it is not for me to question the intensity of the attachments they have to their places. At the moment I am inclined to think, however, that it might be better to avoid drawing a word from te ao Māori to name a relationship to places which we now call 'ours' but which, in many cases, have been prised away from Māori.

For the same reason, I wax and wane on the reciting of pepeha. Right now I'm in a wane phase, ill at ease with claiming an affiliation to a mountain that stands watch over and a river that runs through the confiscated land on which my ancestors made their way in this place. I know there are ways around this, but at the moment it does not feel right for me to claim anything up there on the Coast. That seems like something I should quietly forgo.

I did both of these things once — speak the word and the pepeha — and may do so again. That I choose not to just at the moment has nothing to do with others' views. It is simply what feels right at this point — this waystation — in the interior process of getting from here to there.

I may well be wrong on both counts. English has few or no means of conveying the expanses contained within 'tūrangawaewae' and 'pepeha', and most Pākehā I know hold those words as gifts from te ao Māori and use them with gratitude. But that is the thing about seeing objects rather than categories. The former are specific, particular and personal. They have contexts. The latter are less intimate and more distant, and are only loosely tied, if at all, to this or that set of circumstances. My story is not yours, and nor will be the approach I take to figuring out where I stand. You will make up your own mind about both.

It makes sense to frame this issue — of how to reconcile what we know of the past that came before our present — as a puzzle rather than a contradiction, because while the latter are often beyond resolution the former are things that can generally be solved. Tricky, sure; hard, without question. But I think it can be done, eventually, if we have a method that will get us from a known here to an as-yet unknown there. Especially if what we see between the two is a bridge, not a chasm.

8.

Doing
Stuff

THE GERMAN WRITER W. G. SEBALD DRILY observes that there are 'many difficulties to be reckoned with in the recollection of things'.[1] For some amongst the unsettled, a reckoning with the past and a growing awareness of the reality of the historical foundations on which Pākehā stand in this place generates shame. Despair, too, that there seems so little people can do to put things right.

Then Marguerite sends me a quote from an Australian author, Alice Procter, which sorts things out nicely. Procter is interested in the objects looted by colonial adminstrations which now fill museums. Substitute 'New Zealand' for 'Australia' and she might as well be talking to us:

> I am hyperaware of my own position as a product of empire: a White person whose family took part in the invasion and colonization of Australia, displacing the Indigenous nations who were already there. I do not believe guilt is inherited, but responsibility is, and there is nobody alive today whose existence has not been shaped by colonialist, racist forces. That is a legacy we all live with, and we should all deal with the

consequences. If you have benefitted, then soaking yourself in remorse and guilt does not help anyone. What you can do, though, is ask constantly how you have felt those benefits. At whose expense were they gained?[2]

The questions Procter leaves hanging for we 'products of empire' are: What do we do about that? How do we deal with those consequences? What do the relevant boots on the ground look like? And if notions of responsibility seem too diffuse and the scale of it all too daunting, the American writer Rebecca Solnit is on hand to help out, reminding us that 'the particulars are always challenging the general'.[3] I take this to mean that it is possible to act, even if — perhaps most especially if — it is at the level of our own small stories. Leave the big-picture stuff to the politicians, iwi leaders, judges and officials: our business is with what is right in front of us.

The compulsion to 'do something about it' animates nearly all of the people who have contributed their stories to this book. For them, knowing more of their family histories is not an exercise in 'borrowed nostalgia for an unremembered' time.[4] It is not even a task to be done for its own sake.

There is purpose and intent here; an appetite to learn, not just to ensure that the 'received version of history [is] retold from a more balanced and truthful perspective', as Marguerite put it (although that too), but in order to Do Stuff. At times, what that stuff might be is far from clear; figuring out what we can contribute may well entail an awful lot of fumbling around and ballsing up while possible responses come into focus. One thing is clear, however, and that is the wish to be a part of whatever comes next.

Here is some of what people have done and are doing. Quite a bit of it has happened in full public view. 'As president of the Wellington Teachers College Social Club,' someone recalls, 'I, along with the president of our Student Association, initiated the student protest in Wellington which morphed into "No Maoris No Tour". (Yes, Michael King got the origins of this wrong in his history of New Zealand.) We were standing at the urinal in the Wellington Teachers College when he asked me "What do you think about this tour?" That question started our actions that got the ball rolling and developed into a major student protest.' (Twenty years later this same person was on Tukapa Street in New Plymouth, facing off against 'busloads of semi- if not fully inebriated Waikato supporters who, having been cheated of their game in Hamilton, loyally followed Ces Blazey's boys to New Plymouth' to watch the 1981 Springboks.)

People also take action in workplaces and other institutional contexts. Joe kicked off Whakatūpato, a firearms safety programme for marae and rural Māori communities, and was invited to Maungapōhatu, in the heart of Tūhoe country, to speak. This was in 2012: court action that followed the 2007 police raids in Te Urewera was still live and emotions were raw.[5] Joe was Pākehā police, and it was a significant moment in his career.[6]

Some among his staff wondered what the big deal was, so he prepared a PowerPoint presentation. He sent me the slides, and the first one includes the following: 'Maungapōhatu is the "sacred heart" and mountain of Tūhoe — home fires have burned here since occupation by Māori'; 'Tūhoe did not sign the Treaty of Waitangi, did not want to sell their land under Government conditions, and had massive confiscations and repeated incursion into their territory'; 'The hurt remains'; and, pointedly, 'To be invited as a Pākehā is a privilege'.

Joe's colleagues learned of the confiscation of 125,000 acres of Tūhoe whenua in 1866; the enforced land survey of 1893; the harassment of the prophet Rua Kēnana and his arrest by 57 police at Maungapōhatu on 2 April 1916. There was much he had to get through — a whole history of colonial belligerence towards the People of the Mist told in just 19 slides. But Joe had done his historical homework and got the message across: it was a very big deal indeed, the invitation to Maungapōhatu.

Susan Elizabeth talks of her experiences in a different institution, the Congregation of Our Lady of the Missions. We Catholics know these nuns as the RNDMs, the acronym taken from the French: les Religieuses de Notre Dame des Missions. The order originated in Lyon, as did other Catholic orders that have been active in Aotearoa, including the Marists, who provided the first priestly workforce in this country.

In the 1980s, Susan Elizabeth tells me, the RNDMs dug down into the titles lying behind each of the properties they held, most of which were in Te Wai Pounamu. (Coincidentally, in a post-police incarnation, Joe has done much the same thing, researching and publishing 'the history of land the Church was looking to sell and supporting a financial norm requiring consultation with Māori before doing so'.)

They were searching for confiscated land or for land gifted by Māori but used for other purposes. There were no signs of either, but the nuns nevertheless saw matters needing to be put right: acting on guidance from Ngāi Tahu, a sizeable donation was made to support the establishment of the iwi's archives.

And then there are the acts undertaken at or close to home, and which sometimes quietly find their way out into the wider world. These ones I find compelling for being intimate and private — for who would notice were they not to happen?

David discovered an ancestor who had been a member of the AC, one thing led to another, and now Dorothy and he have set about digitising the AC Description Book, all 240 densely annotated pages of flowing copperplate, much of it faded and virtually all of it difficult to decipher. The book contains the name, place of birth, occupation, age, height, complexion, hair colour, eye colour, distinguishing marks, marital status, religion, and the dates on which every person who ever served in the AC signed on and off. There is also room in the Description Book for miscellaneous remarks, of which there are A Lot. David and Dorothy have taken on a mammoth task, which will be of inordinate value to those seeking to understand the composition of a hybrid military-police force which, between 1866 and 1886, was tasked with imposing 'the norms of the conqueror upon the conquered'.[7]

Another New Plymouth resident, who had taught in the northern Hawke's Bay settlement of Nūhaka between 1963 and 1967, 'became distressed at the sight of very able Māori children underperforming in schools', so he chose to return to university to write 'a thesis exploring our teachers' inability to relate to those kids because of their lack of knowledge and undervaluing of te ao Māori'. It's striking that he placed responsibility for doing the right thing firmly on himself and other teachers. The kids were not the issue here.

There are many ways of giving back. In the mid-1930s Marguerite's father had been gifted a piupiu by the community at Mōkai, near Taupō, where he was head teacher at the local school. A couple of years ago Marguerite arranged for the piupiu to return home after 90 years away, seeing 'a line weaving its way back from this to my grandmother's decision to get involved with Arowhenua Māori'. She is also supporting the restoration of Holy Trinity Church at Arowhenua, the same church her grandmother once raised funds for.[8]

There are layers to this story, and while the church is the focus, the shadow of the land is also visible. In the 1930s the Arowhenua community was energetically seeking to engage the government in the resolution of land claims. 'Two months after my grandmother founded and began leading the Māori Ladies Guild in 1929,' Marguerite explains, 'Sir Apirana Ngata, the minister for native affairs, Mr Makitanara, the MP for Southern Māori, and Chief Judge Jones of the Native Land Court met at Arowhenua to address the on-going land claim issue.

'My grandmother could in no way have been ignorant of this. She knew of their land issues. It was a constant point of discussion on the marae and the wives of men on the rūnanga were those she knew and was friends with, and who would know her own farm was really their land originally. I have to wonder if it discomforted her.'

Marguerite has made clear her view that Ellen Foxon's involvement with the guild and the church was a way of atoning for the Foxons' possession of farms that had once been Ngāi Tahu land. So there is a second thread in her story, this one connecting her own actions with those of her grandmother 90 years later: one of Ellen Foxon's descendants continues to acknowledge the origins of the land on which her family established itself in this place by contributing to the restoration of the Holy Trinity Church.

John pauses and looks closely at a fragment of memory that floats into view as he is mulling over an Australian road trip with his grandson Ben. His wife, Trudi, has recently died and it seems to John that a trip to Tasmania, where Trudi's ancestors John and Bridget Kelly were transported, might be a way of introducing Ben to that aspect of his past. One thing leads to another and John starts shifting up through the gears of time and memory, producing a wee gem of a family history that does not shy away from the hard stuff. Not a jot of it. Looks it right in the eye, in fact.

John's efforts, and those of others who have painstakingly added historical details to received family wisdoms that had long since been discarded, is a form of bearing witness. This, too, is a way of acting in the present and may be pretty much all that is possible, particularly if the land or other resources that might once have flowed into our families through the machinations of the colonial state have since drained away.

But bearing witness on the basis of a new appreciation of our people's history in this place is not abstract or obtuse. It requires taking a public position on the matter of this country's understanding of itself; more than that, it means we need to step into the political maelstrom in a direct and personal way. Bearing witness is a decidedly active thing to do.

Reflecting on what these people have done, it occurs to me that there need be no association between the size of an act and its power: a small gesture is not to be casually dismissed on the basis of its scale, and the intimate may be every bit as consequential as the immense. Small stages (dinner tables) can be harder to work than grand arenas (parliaments, executives and court rooms), and while the sense that one person cannot achieve much can be overwhelming, small acts like these can, in time, be of consequence.

Word gets out; stories get around; family members want to know more; people encounter ideas or angles or information or facts or beliefs or thoughts or views or positions or perspectives they had not previously considered; different conversations are had; things start to shift and change. Slowly. Perhaps.

Doing stuff involves talking about stuff. Conventional wisdom has it that talking is a form of not doing, and is best dispensed with in favour of immediate and vigorous activity. But Pericles, the great Athenian leader, knew a thing or two about the risks of this approach. In a eulogy to the Athenian dead delivered in the first year of the Peloponnesian War, he says approvingly of the Athenian way that it is 'not debate that is a hindrance to action'; rather, the problem is 'not to be instructed by debate before the time comes for action'.[9]

We have to start somewhere, and sometimes the talking begins with a question. Aidan gets going by asking himself: 'Why the silence on how my people, who arrived here as poor immigrants, came to acquire the land they held?' That is perhaps the biggest question of all, because to answer it we need to embark on an excursion with no map, no manual and no idea where we might end up. Aidan's question is the small-story equivalent of a large-scale expedition into the unknown.

Sometimes the talking takes the shape of stories. Gillian's novels can be read as attempts to write out the discomfort and the unease. In her first novel, *A Red Silk Sea*, the land carries the stories of the violence that took place upon it and that continues to erupt in the lives of those living on it today.

Gillian's words — which take issue with the comfortable notion that the past can be kept conveniently out of sight in the corner, just over there — are not always welcomed. She recalls the bemusement and disbelief among parishioners who attended a reading from *A Red Silk Sea* organised by a local priest. Surely, they said, it could not have been like that? But it was.

Whatever its form, the talking takes place in many different rooms. The veteran of the anti-racism protests of the 1960s and 1980s tells me that he has finally 'matured to the point where I will challenge negative talk about Māori at a dinner party'. He is ahead of me on this one. I think I'm doing okay on the pronunciation of Māori words, but the niceties of polite Pākehā conversation are so deeply embedded in me that I still struggle to confront casual racism. This same person helped design and facilitate decolonisation seminars in the early 1990s, getting plenty of stick from Pākehā for doing so. He tells me that there are fewer angry words these days.

Some of those rooms are really buses. In 2010 Kiaran's youngest aunt organised a family reunion in New Plymouth. It kicked off with a bus trip around the mountain, and Kiaran remembers 'pointing out to my sister when we passed Parihaka. She was quite intrigued and wanted to know more. My wife, Sarah, thought I should say a few words, and so, being a very accommodating spouse, I took the bus PA system and said that although we were celebrating Andrew and Honora, we should spare a thought for the original people on the land and that it (the land) had been mostly confiscated. This was met with very muted applause, led largely by my wife.'

Some of those rooms can be found in starkly contrasting settings. 'Granny's two grandfathers built two very different houses in the nineteenth century,' Gillian tells me. 'John Bryce built a mansion of tōtara and rimu, 3200 square feet, with a

12-foot stud on both floors, there was an entrance hall, and a parlour of ballroom proportions, where a number of family weddings took place. The dining room table seated 20 people. The bedrooms were described as being on a generous scale, many with fireplaces, and the kitchen was fitted with a stove eight feet long. It was built in the 1870s, but less than 100 years later, the foundations had sunk, and the house was demolished.'

Her Granny's father, on the other side of the family, 'was born in a mud-and-stud cottage built by his father in Robin Hood Bay, not far from, and not long after, what happened at Wairau in 1843'. Gillian, her sister and their respective partners visited this cottage a couple of years ago. There was another couple there that day, 'a woman descended from Rangitāne o Wairau, and her Welsh husband. Her people had lived in the bay before Ngāti Toa arrived, and as we exchanged our family stories, we all thought how lovely it would be to put the kettle on, sit around the table and simply talk. The place had a way of invoking such things.'

As it happens, Gillian knows something of Rangitāne history, including what she has read in a book by former secretary of Maori and Island affairs and Rangitāne historian Jock McEwen, a Pākehā and one of her father's cousins. The men's 'maternal grandmothers were both daughters of Anne and John Bryce . . . [b]ut I did not know of Jock until very recently. I did not know that he had grown up near the Aorangi marae, had known the Durie family, learnt to speak te reo and to carve, or that he became a founding member of Ngāti Pōneke and a tohunga whakairo, set up a carving school for Māori prisoners, and carved the matapihi at the Pipitea marae and the pou standing at the entrance of the Michael Fowler Centre, amongst many other things. I did not know any of this because I did not want to know anything to do with the Bryce family. That, too, was a loss.'

And so the words that we try to put around these difficult things matter. And who is to say that, having read my words here, you will not strike up your own conversation about them with someone else. Your words and theirs will swirl together, pile up, cohere into something larger. What you say will be heard by the other — agreed with and accepted, or contested and pushed back against, or misunderstood (for what is heard is not always what was said) and perhaps batted away.

The exchange could end in frustration, or worse (especially if it is with one of Carolyn Morris's 'not-knowers' or Charles Mills's 'non-knowers'), but it might also be that through it the two of you build new meaning, and the way in which you see and make sense of the world will subtly shift. The words will have carried you forward, each enquiry displacing what was there before.[10]

It is this sense of propulsion away from the status quo that counts. In time the momentum will be manifest in more material ways, and while the contours of those consequences cannot be immediately visible, what *is* clear is that energy has replaced inertia or, worse, entropy. Chances are that this is a positive step, if the texture of the energy matches the intent behind it. So, yes, the encounters with words matter. They are how we change the future.

Take Win's advice on this. She is, she says, 'convinced that I need to find out the details, as much as possible, of my forebears' history. I have to accept that their roles and actions were theirs but that I am complicit in them by not knowing and admit my regret in that.' Heed her counsel. Learn your small story. Know your place (literally). Fill in the silences with words.

Just as negative space in a piece of art provides focus and structure to the work, so too choosing not to do something can be a form of doing something. Joe, for example, suggests it is high time we 'acknowledge the past honestly and get on with levelling the playing field for Māori in today's complex world. That mostly means getting out of their way as they fix things brilliantly themselves.'

Resolving to get out of the way; deciding not to take up space; opting to stand in the metaphorical wings; holding our peace; listening (especially to other stories that may be quietly burbling away alongside our own) rather than speaking; choosing silence over voice; denying ourselves something (anything) rather than claiming a right to it — these are all forms of action, and no less powerful than their obverse. Colly, one of Owen Marshall's fictional characters, had the gift of seeing 'space not emptiness'.[11] Just so.

The people whose voices are heard in this book are doing the best they can, quietly getting on with the business of getting things straight. Of bringing balance back into their worlds. They're like the ones out in the kitchen at a big family gathering, putting in the unseen (and often unsung) hard yards. No one professes to have answers to everything, or even to many things. Most would say they really have no answers at all, but I take issue with them on this. More than anything, perhaps, what we need are people who can ask questions.

Some issues are especially gnarly. What do you do, for instance, if you live in a house that sits on land that was confiscated from mana whenua during the New Zealand Wars? Justine won't be alone in being unsure what to do about this, although she may be one of the few who 'would welcome conversations with others who are in a similar situation'.

The point is that she is asking the question. And at the origin of many momentous things there is a well-crafted question.

In no particular order. Sort your attitude out | do the right thing | including doing your historical due diligence | observe He Rā Maumahara | get the PowerPoint right | give things back | give things to | give things away | give people access | get your organisation's strategy right | tell a different story | by getting the family story straight | including by reading 3000 entries in PapersPast to find the lost farms | and by reading about colonial history | ask the right questions | have the awkward conversation | listen | especially to Māori | then listen some more | grab the PA on the bus and say some things | but not others | help get the church back into shape | call out the racists at the table | face the front | get out of the way | speak out | and also hold your peace | make space | organise protests | as well as go on protests | point your family trust in the right direction | take the AC's records to the people | do a thesis and take that to the people, too | give a damn | read | especially read up on what happened where you live | write | especially write family histories that include colonial context | as well as other stuff you'd rather not know about | take responsibility | update your courses | turn shame into action | bear witness | tell the truth | light the flame for another.

It's not #LandBack, perhaps, but it certainly isn't nothing.

9.
Becoming

W HEN MARGARET MEAD AND JAMES BALDWIN were sitting on that New York stage in 1970, one of the many things they talked about was the part the past might play not just in understanding the present but also in building a more dignified future.

The search for the traces of our pasts takes place in the present. We need to be mindful, of course, of the ways in which things we are familiar with colour our understandings of those which we can never intimately apprehend. But I have come to think that the reverse process is even more important. As do others to whom I listen and with whom I talk. We are finding that those traces — what the writer Peter Wells called the 'dropped hairpins' of our pasts — have a way of setting to work on the sense we make of the present.[1]

When we learn a new fact about our history — a family ancestor participating in the invasion of Parihaka over here; family farms on land obtained by dubious means over there — it becomes part of the interior prism through which we see and live in the world. Having learned this, we can't unlearn it. It is now part of that great swirl of ourself that we carry about, fashioning what we see, whether we wish it to or not. The South Road now seems different to me; these days Gillian sees Pākaraka where perhaps once she saw Maxwell; Marguerite is supporting the refurbishment of a church she did not know existed a year or so ago; Ōpōtiki does not look the way it once did to John.

Those inflections have a bearing on what happens when choices must be made — whether to engage in or avoid that awkward conversation; to read about or ignore the latest report on a Treaty settlement; to listen to that item on colonisation or to spin the digital dial. And in turn each of these decisions contributes to the unfurling of future moments. Finding stuff out can change how you do stuff.

As she so often does, Rachel Buchanan takes us to the nub of the matter when she speaks of 'grasp[ing] the hem of a new kind of knowledge that is about not what was but what could be'.[2] I like Buchanan's strong, gentle image: knowledge not a weapon to be wielded in a contest for supremacy (nor something over which dominion can ever be established), but a fabric that clothes, warms and protects. This is knowledge as warp and weft; an understanding of a future way of being that emerges from and in concert with memories of past ways of doing.

Nothing about this is inevitable, of course. If I shun or turn away from those difficult aspects of my past, or reduce my backstory to some stock pioneer orthodoxy, then that is what will inform my present and set the trajectory of my future.

In that future the South Road is simply a road and Maxwell is just another small Taranaki town. That future is known and will never change. But if I choose otherwise — if I reach for the hem of a different garment of knowledge — what lies ahead remains unwoven. Historical retrospection is powerful because it can shape what we become.

Here is another way of making this point. Rachel Buchanan's people own a piece of land just off the Eltham Road, near Ōpunake in south Taranaki. But she needs to ask the permission of a Pākehā farmer to drive across a property confiscated from her tūpuna by the colonial state to get to the sliver they managed to hang on to.[3] The status of being 'an invited guest on [her] own land' seems likely to endure for some time to come.[4] This is past, present and future all rolled into one unholy mess. It must be pretty hard to move on from. I don't think I could do it.

Yeats's 'The Second Coming' — 'Things fall apart; the centre cannot hold' — swims back into view when I recall the sense of emotional slippage that followed on the heels of finding out that my great-grandfather had participated in the invasion of Parihaka and farmed on confiscated land.[5] Others, too, have had their own experiences of the slow collapse of old ways of sense-making. Marguerite has reflected at length on what it has taken to deconstruct her 'view of my personal or family history, what I have learned about my country at school, [and] what my society tells me is historical fact'. She also frankly acknowledges that 'when faced with the falling apart it is hard yakka to begin the process of reconstruction, let alone see it through — assuming that is possible. We may have to live with the ambiguity for a long time.'

Joan Didion has written about this interior experience of implosion. Her words have helped me make sense of what happens after the initial unstitching has taken place, as things regroup in a sort of internal, secular second coming

— albeit one that has nothing to do with exoneration, little to do with redemption and quite a bit to do with trying to put our understanding of our past back together in ways that demonstrate greater fidelity to what actually took place.[6]

I don't believe these processes of private reappraisal can be reduced to the inner lives of particular people. They do not simply begin and end with those in whom they take place. Things connect. Accumulate. Cohere. The questioning — What really took place? Who benefited from what occurred? Were things really as I have always thought them to be? — is of necessity intensely personal in the first instance, but the consequences of confronting the questions can radiate out and resonate with others.

In her 1967 essay 'Slouching Towards Bethlehem', Didion talked of a national centre that was failing to hold; a social compact — an assemblage of norms, mores and received wisdoms — that was rapidly unravelling. Didion was writing about the US, and the sense of malaise she conveyed did not necessarily apply in Aotearoa at that time. However, there is something in her words — the sense of a fundamental shift taking place — that I hope speaks to our experience as we slowly turn to face a past from which many of us have averted our eyes for too long.

Sure, the indifference, incomprehension and anger which Didion saw can also be seen in the way some people react to the questions being asked here of established ways of (not) thinking about colonisation. But there is also a growing willingness to look again, and more closely, at that legacy, and with an understanding that 'our current moment is inflected with remnants of earlier histories that have been dismantled, rearranged and built upon over time'.[7]

While some rail against what is emerging, others embrace that which is taking shape. For those of us who are in any way tethered to the ongoing legacy of colonisation in this country, it is certainly possible to ignore this uncomfortable history. But it is not really possible to break the tie. Like it or not, it is there: there is nobody here whose life has not been shaped by colonisation. The very land we walk, work, love, live and die on has been the front line of empire-building. It still is. That is a legacy we all live with, and the only thing at issue is how — or whether — we choose to deal with it.

The people who contributed their small stories to this book are cracking on with the business of rising to that challenge. They are not seeking to deny any personal association with colonisation; they are treating that past not as 'a phase to outgrow or a problem to be superseded so much as a set of relationships that persist' and need to be understood.[8] They are in the business of what Avril Bell calls entering 'into a relationship with colonisation rather than being redeemed from implication in it'.[9] Of comprehending and living with it, rather than endlessly trying to keep the damn thing at bay.

Denying this relationship simply requires maintaining the omertà. Acknowledging it is harder, because honesty and backbone are called for. The work starts with people like Justine, who is conscious that 'realising that colonisation isn't just something that happened 200 years ago, but that it's an ongoing process which I am contributing to, is a difficult thing to sit with'.

And it continues with people like Jane, who is prepared to share an experience from a te reo Māori course she completed some years ago. In it she 'encountered Māori classmates who had an abiding anger at our colonial history. It reminded me of a classmate from Puniho Pā, when I was in Year 3, who commented scathingly (and correctly) that "all you [Pākehā] stick together" when a decision went against her. Her writing was untidy, and the teacher interpreted a six as a zero in a maths test. I was asked by the teacher for an opinion. I wrongly, but perhaps understandably given the biased behaviour we were being subjected to, sided with the teacher. These incidents, together with bits and pieces from family life began to niggle: I felt more and more that there was something wrong in the acknowledged story, the assumption that everything was OK. But the assumptions have been based on inaccurate information. The more we can do to fill the silences, to correct the stories, the better.'

They do not abjure their pasts, my collaborators, but neither do they understand them simply as 'the process by which the present was attained', one which only ever held the germ of the present they find themselves in.[10] Instead, they are figuring out how to reach an accommodation with their histories. This is not easy to do, but it begins with not dismissing, avoiding or erasing the hard parts of our past. It gets under way when, as John so neatly puts it and Jane so frankly demonstrates, people decide to become 'part of the not forgetting'.

Constitutional lawyer and activist Moana Jackson once wrote that 'the new stories [of the colonisers] never found an easy place in this land. Rather, they sat uneasily upon it like the new place names and fences that were being strung across the new private properties. They were intruder stories on a land that needed no such embellishment.'[11] What's going on here, I think, is that some of those intruder stories are being questioned and reworked by the children of those who first told them.

✳

It sounds deceptively straightforward. Perhaps at the start it is. Nearly all of the sources I used in an attempt to end my own stay in the historical dementia wing were just an internet query away, or lying on a shelf in the archives of the New Zealand state. Sometimes it felt as if those records were hiding from me; at others that they were simply waiting to be found. Either way, they were often just a click away.

But getting hold of the raw material is the easy part. The difficulties come when we need to make sense of what it tells us about our background (and therefore ourselves). For that part we need help. In particular, we need the time to sit, read and imagine a picture of the wider context in which the lives revealed through the archival record were lived.

We realise that we need Rachel Buchanan, Joanna Kidman and Vincent O'Malley; Judith Binney, Claudia Orange and Danny Keenan; Hazel Riseborough, Anne Salmond and Dinah Hawken; the Waitangi Tribunal and PapersPast. (Sometimes we also need Fred Vargas, whose advice 'to lie flat on top of it, if you [aren't] to plunge up to your waist in its quicksands' is worth following when we get bogged down in the detail.)[12] We need patience and fortitude; poetry, prose and a good internet connection. Most of all, we have to learn how to be still with the discomfort that comes — inexorably and inevitably — when it dawns on us that foundation stories we hold dear are as mist on a cold winter's morning; that our ancestors were involved in events that brought pain, suffering and loss to other people; and that we have gained from what others have lost.

When that happens, and it will, Avril Bell's insight that the descendants of colonial settlers carry the 'twinned desires for belonging and for redemption from the status of coloniser' will make perfect sense.[13] Whether we will know how to deal with that contradiction is another matter.

Beyond gently encouraging others to think about their own small stories, it is not my place to suggest to anyone else that they should do this, that or the other thing. There is no manual, no 'best practice' for this work in progress. There is, at most, a disposition (to set aside ideas about universal ways of being and think about particular ones) and an intent (a willingness to walk into the shade), but beyond that it is a matter of being able to sit with the ambiguity and lack of clarity, and to avoid the temptation to push for resolution (much less redemption). It is neither comfortable nor easy to 'dwell with the pieces', but for now it is probably enough for most of us to be getting on with.[14]

I have learned a great deal about this from Gillian, Kiaran, Marguerite and the rest, who understand that '[u]nless the past and the future [are] made part of the present by memory and intention', as Ursula Le Guin once said, 'there [is], in human terms, no road, nowhere to go'.[15] They have found that road, and are demonstrating how to travel it. This is not the 'moving on' of those unable, or unwilling, to look our colonial history in the eye, but a 'moving with'.

This is moving ahead with the knowledge of challenging events that took place in our pasts (not setting them aside); with an awareness of what those events have meant for the people on the receiving end (rather than a dogged refusal to countenance that history has consequences); and with a willingness to see things afresh (not an insistence that the dementia wing of colonial history is the place to be).

And if it is the case that 'individual and collective memories evolve in tandem', then perhaps there are grounds for optimism and hope to be found in these people's willingness to tell their small stories.[16] For although these stories have been the focus in this book — the everyday acts and omissions of people such as Bridget and John Kelly, Ellen Foxon, John Bryce and Andrew Gilhooly; of William Green and Frank the allrounder — in the end it is a collective, consensual culture of silence that keeps us all from moving ahead.

The minutiae of the lives of the people who came before us matter, no question, but this thing is systemic. As long as enough of us choose to keep quiet about what happened to mana whenua from Taranaki, the Waikato, Ōpōtiki, Te Wai Pounamu and elsewhere, and to maintain the fiction that none of us is in any way responsible for the consequences of that damage, then we're all good. Sweet as. No worries. This is how it goes: if we all keep quiet or stay obdurately angry, then the system keeps ticking over quietly.

Of course, the reverse can also happen. We might start sorting out our small stories, as those who've told theirs here are doing, and the culture of silence may start withering away. We may come to realise, as Aidan already has, that 'the embracing of tikanga does not come at the expense of Pākehā and instead creates a much more special country'. It's up to us, really.

I think about this business of sorting stuff out as I walk around a museum in Nagasaki. An exhibition by the Spanish painter and sculptor Manuel Franquelo is on, *The Language of Things*. I'm not good with art unless it's fairly literal, and struggle to make sense of Franquelo's work. What does catch my eye, however, is the text at the start of the exhibition, written by the

French philosopher Bruno Latour. One particular paragraph stands out, in which Latour suggests that 'the language of texture can be heard over the superficial language of shape' in Franquelo's photography.

I'm about as good with Latour as I am with modern art, but I think he is saying that whereas the shape of an object is either one thing or another — sharp or fuzzy; crisp or blurred; this or that — such easy dichotomies cannot capture texture. Texture contains the stuff of lives lived, and for that the language of scratches, spatters, stains and smears is required.

I've thought about Latour's words since, and it occurs to me that the general acceptance of the overall shape of the classical settler-colonial story in Aotearoa New Zealand — the endless recital of the pattern of leaving there and arriving here; of working hard and prevailing over the land; of building a better life than the one left behind — is a bit of a problem. That template gives a reassuringly familiar, recognisable order to our small Pākehā stories, but it also tends to be fixed. Its contours are stable, settled and hard to change, and do not readily permit the addition of other narrative elements — especially if they change the shape of the story. No surprise, really, that Kiaran lost his audience on the bus when he departed from the script. That other unsettling stuff is not what we really want to hear: what we want are the greatest hits.

Furthermore, for as long as there is a canonical shape to our settler-colonial epics, it is difficult to add certain kinds of texture to them. The shape is what does most of the work demanded of those foundational narratives, and that is to claim our place in and on this land. Their texture — the specifics of your version of the story or mine — is not unimportant, but is often subordinate to the job at hand.

Then I wonder what Latour might have made of the efforts of those around whose stories this book has meandered. I like to think that he would have entirely approved of their awkward questions, difficult conversations and dogged attempts to get to grips with matters that make them uneasy — seeing in all of this the labour of people determined to change the shape of, and then to etch, daub, scribble or slather more texture onto their small stories.

Robert Macfarlane has wryly observed that the English were wont 'to grid [the world] and to girdle it with maps'.[17] (The Royal Commission on The Confiscated Lands Inquiry and Maori Prisoners' Trials Act 1879 got there ahead of him, noting that 'there is nothing so good as laying out the lines upon the ground'.)[18] One such, an 1871 sketch map of the 'Province of Taranaki and Coast Line to Wanganui', is tucked away amongst old parliamentary papers dealing with the construction of roads in the North Island.[19] It is a fascinating artefact, mostly for what it omits.

For a start, the Cape Egmont lighthouse is missing (it would be another decade before it was hauled ashore at the bottom of the Cape Road), and there is no road linking Ōkato and Ōpunake. In fact, there is not much of anything — apart from a great deal of empty white space waiting to be filled in. But it is a tricky thing, this map, and we have to be wary of it, for like many of the maps sketched by English surveyors in the colonised places of the world, the unmarked spaces obliterate the lands, estates, forests and fisheries that belonged to and were known intimately by those who lived there before the

British and their helpmeets arrived. In so doing, they also erase the people themselves.

In time, of course, as the colonial frontiers moved inland and the names of British soldiers, surveyors and statesmen were splattered on the maps like so much 'imperial graffiti', even the white spaces would disappear.[20] In 1871, however, what the map shows is not what was there, but what the colonisers imagined was not there. There is no texture. Yet.

I came across this map when, with Kelvin Day's considerable help, I was patching together the history of the South Road that appeared in an earlier chapter, and I find myself coming back to it again as I reach the end of this book. It is the absences that draw my eye: the depiction of the whenua on which Māori had lived and died for generations as a void; the rendering as unknown that which was deeply familiar. And this prompts me to reflect on the inner maps each of us carries of the landscape of our memories.

There are prominent cartographical features on the imaginary charts we use to navigate to and through our pasts, the equivalent of mountains and rivers, of coastlines, forests and plains. But there are also uncharted expanses, although they differ from those of the 1871 sketch of the Taranaki coast. In the private maps of our interiors the silence often falls in places that were once regularly traversed but which have since been abandoned — because of trauma, shame, carelessness or neglect; because for some reason it serves our purposes to do so — and are now avoided lest the fretful sleep of the monsters still slumbering there be disturbed. On our maps of the mind these are the places we do not wish to tread.

I think of the small stories recounted here as expeditions by the unsettled into this terra incognita of memory. It is hard to walk off a map these days, but in our interior landscape we are on our own. These are as much journeys of recovery as they are odysseys of discovery. Each painstaking attempt to ink in a sliver of white is an act of reclamation; a little more texture is added through the application of splashes of historical colour.

More to the point, the voyagers — the people met in these pages and the others we share this country with — are not so much walking off the map of memory as journeying back into it. They are taking up Emily Wilson's challenge to find the beginning, because they know that it is by taking the old ways winding through the forgotten places of our pasts that they might yet chart a truer course into the future.

Postscript

Lunch in Waikanae

ARLY IN DECEMBER 2022 I DRIVE FROM
Te Whārangi Foxton Beach to Waikanae to have lunch
with two nuns. This is not the sort of thing I often do.
Susan Elizabeth lives in Whangārei and is visiting her friend
Barbara, who grew up in Eltham but has been on the Kāpiti
Coast for 20 years. Both women are members of the Sisters
of Mercy. My mother's oldest sister, Cath, was also an RNDM.
Barbara knew Cath very well; Susan Elizabeth met her only
briefly a couple of times before she died 30 years ago.

Lunch is good. The talk is better, ranging over all sorts of
Catholic ground. They have lived full lives of service, these
women, service to their God and to those with whom they live
in this world. In Bangladesh, Ethiopia and Sāmoa; Ōpōtiki and
Te Wai Pounamu. It pays to listen to them carefully.

Sometimes in a conversation we are fortunate to be gifted
wisdom. In my experience this happens rarely. Today it
happens twice. The first offering comes when the three of us
are reflecting on the shape the order is in as the vocations fall
away and the older sisters pass on. I wonder if this is cause for
sadness, but Barbara says it feels as if she — and they — are
'coming to completion'.

I have never heard this phrase before and am immediately taken by it. It is full and round. It feels replete and speaks of work accomplished and lives lived well. The RNDMs have done their job, Susan Elizabeth explains; the 'cheap labour' the nuns provided in religious schools is no longer needed; that purpose is at an end. There is no rancour, just a quiet, contemplative ease.

I ask: What takes its place? What comes now? They think on this for a little while and then both agree that they are 'in search of letting things go'. I am struck a second time, for these six words contain a life. They elide time. A quest is often a search for something in the future, while what Barbara and Susan Elizabeth are seeking is a letting go of things gathered in the past. This is an ending without loss, an unencumbering, a setting aside in order to become something other. It is not what most people generally go in search of.

I drive home thinking about what it might mean for me and other Pākehā to come to completion. I think that if we are to do so — if we are to learn how to live in and with our small stories of colonisation — we need to let some things go. Old ways of knowing and thinking. Old anxieties and old behaviours. Old stories. We need to put some things aside that we might become something new. I have no idea what shape that new thing might take. For now, it is enough simply to reach out, seeking the hem of that unknown garment.

Notes

Chapter 1. Find the Beginning

1   Emily Wilson (ed.), *The Odyssey: Homer* (New York: W. W. Norton & Co., 2019), 105.
2   As can be the way with such things, there are several slightly different spellings of the village in which my great-grandfather was born. I shall use 'Ballynagreanagh' throughout, but the contemporary Irish sources contain other variations.
3   The prefix 'Royal' was not added until 1867, when it was bestowed as an expression of the Queen's gratitude for the Constabulary's role in quelling the Fenian Rising on 5 and 6 March 1867, so for the present they remain the Irish Constabulary.
4   Following the invasion, pass laws restricting Māori movements into, out of and within Parihaka were enforced. Waitangi Tribunal, *Taranaki Report: Kaupapa Tuatahi* (Wai 143) (Wellington: 1996), 237.
5   Rachel Buchanan, *The Parihaka Album: Lest We Forget* (Wellington: Huia, 2009), 39.
6   Not long before this book went to print, a curious thing happened. In *The Forgotten Coast*, I briefly mention a trophy which, following my grandfather Hugh's death, his family had donated to the Rāhotu rugby club (which he was president of for many years) and which was on the line each time Rāhotu played Ōpunake. I tried, unsuccessfully, to track the thing down. In June 2023, a couple of years after I'd stopped looking, Kelvin Day (author and former tumuaki of the Puke Ariki Museum in New Plymouth) got in touch to tell me that he'd seen something called 'The Andrew and Hugh Gilhooly Rugby Shield' up on TradeMe, the

online auction site. Long-ish story short, that shield now sits in my office, thanks to the generosity of Aaron from Ōpunake, who had hauled it out of a rubbish skip in Waitara and who, on learning that I was descended from both men, decided the shield needed to be back in the family and that I shouldn't pay for it. One other thing: in 1995 the Rāhotu, Ōpunake and Ōkato clubs merged to form the Coastal Rugby Club — reverting to the same name that appears on the 1881 photo I have of Hugh's father standing with his AC Coastal rugby teammates. That shield is doing some interesting historical work.

7   'Memory' is a slippery term. Israeli cultural historian Alon Confino suggests it encompasses recollections of events that people (individually or collectively) have directly experienced, as well as 'the representation of the past and the making of it into a shared cultural knowledge by successive generations in "vehicles of memory" such as books, films, museums, commemorations, and much else besides'. See Alon Confino, 'Collective Memory and Cultural History: Problems of Method', *American Historical Review* 102, no. 5 (1997): 1386–1403. In this book, I tend towards the second of those understandings.

8   The estimate is from Peter Adds, 'Te Muru me te Raupatu: The Aftermath', in Kelvin Day (ed.), *Contested Ground Te Whenua i Tohea: The Taranaki Wars 1860–1881* (Wellington: Huia, 2010), 255–61.

9   This detail is from the Ngāti Tama Claims Settlement Act 2003. Since 2003 each of the eight Taranaki iwi (Ngāti Tama, Ngāti Ruanui, Ngaa Rauru Kiitahi, Ngāti Mutunga, Ngā Ruahine, Te Ātiawa, Taranaki and, most recently, Ngāti Maru) has negotiated settlements.

10 The lighthouse was hauled north from Mana Island, where its elevation was too high for its beam to have been of much use to coastal shipping.

11 The ban on the fourth estate was only partially successful, with two reporters — including Samuel Croumbie-Brown (or Crombie-Brown) from the *Lyttleton Times* — nipping in around the back of the pā to witness what went on. Vincent O'Malley includes a previously unpublished poem Croumbie-Brown wrote following the invasion in *Voices of the New Zealand Wars He Reo nō ngā Pakanga o Aotearoa* (Wellington: Bridget Williams Books, 2021), 362–65.

12 Buchanan, *The Parihaka Album*, 177.

13 The detail in this paragraph is taken from an untitled document that informed the Waitangi Tribunal's 1996 interim report on Taranaki (Wai I17[g]). From it I also learn that by the early twentieth century the system of occupation licences in Taranaki applied to an area of some 20,367 acres.

14 Reflecting on the impact of colonisation on Māori, Gillian Ranstead, one of those who have made this book possible, suggests that '[i]t is not

difficult to understand how this atomising world might have happened in a modern nation-state founded on fractured, dislocated peoples, on the dishonouring of cultures and traditions'. I think she is onto something.

15 Andrew had purchased the first of the three Gilhooly farms, Section 44 Block 12 Cape Survey District, in 1895. He took out a lease on the second, Section 103 Block 13 Cape Survey District, which was Māori land, in 1902. Kate purchased her own farm, Section 102 Block 12 Cape Survey District (referred to in the archives as Parihaka A), in 1921.

16 Tohu Kākahi and Te Whiti o Rongomai (both of whom were from Taranaki and Te Ātiawa iwi) were the spiritual leaders of Parihaka, which they established in 1866. The sources on both men include Buchanan, *The Parihaka Album*; Danny Keenan, *Te Whiti o Rongomai and the Resistance of Parihaka* (Wellington: Huia, 2015); and Hazel Riseborough, *Days of Darkness: The Government and Parihaka, Taranaki, 1878–1884* (Auckland: Penguin, 2002).

17 *The Forgotten Coast* was published by Massey University Press in 2021.

18 The book was published shortly after the article appeared here: https://tinyurl.com/2p8f4fst.

19 I have no presence on Facebook, Twitter or Instagram, but I gather there was a fair amount of activity on those platforms, too.

20 I imagine the irony of the band's choice of entertainment might have been lost on some. The *Timaru Herald* of 13 February 1867 reported that during the visit Grey spent time at the Arowhenua pā, on which — having demurred when asked to remove the tax on Māori dogs — he pronounced himself 'very glad to meet such a peaceful lot of natives, and congratulated them on their position in contradistinction to some of the Maoris in the North'.

21 As does one of Niall William's characters in his novel *As It Is in Heaven* (London: Picador, 1999), 50.

22 You can see why mana whenua (and some Pākehā, for that matter, including Gillian, Bryce's descendant) successfully campaigned to have the name changed. Hours after they were installed, however, in late January 2023, the new signs informing drivers that they were entering Pākaraka were ripped out (https://tinyurl.com/5n84apy6). But the last time I drove through, in June 2023, the signs were up and intact.

23 Vincent O'Malley examines what occurred at Handley's Woolshed in *Voices from the New Zealand Wars*, 341–45.

24 Elizabeth Strout, *My Name Is Lucy Barton* (New York: Vintage, 2016), 146.

25 The quote is from Kate Grenville, *A Room Made of Leaves* (Melbourne: Text, 2020), 129. The process of gathering people's views for this book is set out in the acknowledgements.

26   Jonathan Gottschall, *The Storytelling Animal: How Stories Make Us Human* (Boston: Houghton Mifflin Harcourt, 2012).

27   I encountered the idea of 'settler stamina' in Avril Bell, 'Building Stamina, Fighting Fragility: The Account of a White Settler "Recovering Racist"', *Ethnicities* 22, no. 5 (2022): 685–704. Bell's article is based on an interview with former New Plymouth mayor Andrew Judd, a self-confessed 'recovering racist', and is full of insights. Highly recommended.

28   The images are from Andrew Garran's *Picturesque Atlas of Australasia*: https://nla.gov.au/nla.obj-1605485403.

29   Keith Ovenden, *Bill and Shirley: A Memoir* (Auckland: Massey University Press, 2020), 162.

30   Ibid., 172.

31   I have opted to leave things as they were originally spelt when quoting from the parliamentary record and from published sources, even if contemporary usage and spelling differ. Apart from where I have specifically indicated otherwise, however, macrons have been added to quotations taken from the correspondence I have received.

32   *New Zealand Parliamentary Debates (NZPD)*, 1879, vol. 34, 621; 797.

33   On the subject of this practice, see Rachel Buchanan, *Te Motunui Epa* (Wellington: Bridget Williams Books, 2022).

34   There are plenty of examples of this, of course, some of which led a Mr Sheehan to observe that 'the whole district [Taranaki] was sown three feet thick with broken pledges and broken promises': see Alfred Cox, *Recollections: Australia, England, Ireland, Scotland, New Zealand* (Christchurch: Whitcombe & Tombs, 1884), 241. And the *Press* (28 December 1891) reported that, during a visit to Kaiapoi, Governor Onslow responded to a request to honour the undertakings the Crown had made to Ngāi Tahu thus: 'It may be that you think you ought to have received more money for your rights in the land you sold, but at the time you were content, and it is the skill and knowledge of my countrymen which has proved the land to be of greater value than was then believed.' This is gaslighting on an epic scale.

35   Raimond Gaita, an Australian political philosopher, coined this term in *A Common Humanity: Thinking About Love and Truth and Justice* (London: Routledge, 2022), but I'd like to thank my friend, the sociologist Avril Bell, for introducing me to it.

36   Alex Calder, *The Settler's Plot: How Stories Take Place in New Zealand* (Auckland: Auckland University Press, 2011), 87.

37   John Bluck, *Becoming Pākehā: A Journey Between Two Cultures* (Auckland: HarperCollins, 2022).

Chapter 2. Small Stories

1   I'm not sure who coined the term 'small stories', but both Avril Bell and
    Catherine Padmore use it to terrific effect. I recommend Bell's 'Moving
    Roots: A "Small Story" of Settler History and Home Places', *Qualitative
    Inquiry* 23, no. 6 (2017): 452–57, and Padmore's 'Telling Home Stories',
    Life Writing 6, no. 2 (2009): 267–78.

2   Robyn Fivush, Helen McAnally and Elaine Reese, 'Family Stories and
    Family Secrets', *Journal of New Zealand Studies* 29 (2019): 20.

3   Sociologist Avril Bell recalls being struck, later in her life, by realising
    that 'the family trees I drew up as a young person all started with the
    ancestor who first came to New Zealand'. (The quote is from her article
    'Reverberating Historical Privilege of a "Middling" Sort of Settler Family',
    Genealogy 4 (2020): 46.) As far as I can recall, my own efforts didn't even
    get that far back but began with my grandparents' generation.

4   In its *Taranaki Report: Kaupapa Tuatahi* (Wai 143) (Wellington: Waitangi
    Tribunal, 1996), the Waitangi Tribunal describes 'the so-called "battle" of
    Waireka on 28 March' as 'a badly coordinated attempt by regular troops
    and local militia to rescue besieged settlers south of New Plymouth'. The
    Tribunal takes issue with the standard representation of the encounter as
    a victory for the colonial government, citing historian James Belich's view
    that Māori casualties were 'grossly exaggerated' in the official record, and
    probably numbered 'about one' rather than the 50 that were reported.

5   You don't always get to learn the detail. In *Fleming Pioneers Recalled:
    1881–1979*, a booklet prepared for a gathering of the Fleming clan in 1979,
    there is a glancing note about how well Richard Fleming — my great-
    grandmother's father, with whom she migrated to New Zealand in 1895
    — 'remembered the unsettled times in Ireland in 1847 and 1848' and
    how he often 'gave interesting accounts of his experiences during that
    troubled period'. Frustratingly, none of those interesting accounts makes
    it into the booklet.

6   As far as John can tell, Bridget did not sign the 1892 Suffrage Petition.
    He knows, however, that in the 1908 election 'one of the candidates,
    James Gow, gave Bridget a ride to the polls. Bridget thanked him before
    informing him that she was not going to vote for him.' Gow lost, so
    Bridget clearly knew what she was about.

7   John researched and wrote *Famine, Land and Children: The Story of
    Bridget and John Kelly of Ōpotoki* following his wife Trudi's death. It is
    a formidable piece of work. Traces of people like Bridget and John Kelly
    linger in the archives of institutions such as courts, police forces, prisons
    and so forth, but finding them is not an easy process and John has done

an uncommonly thorough job of tracking down and building a picture of both of his wife's ancestors. What sets his work apart is his assiduous attention to ensuring that what happens to Bridget and John is placed in historical context: in particular, he weaves their small story into the bigger one of the Waikato War. I owe John a debt for his permission to reproduce parts of his work in these pages.

8   Around a third of the population is thought to have left during what Cornish historians call the 'Great Emigration'. The drift away was strongly gendered: some 45 per cent of men aged between 15 and 24 emigrated during the second half of the nineteenth century, many leaving women and families behind. Lesley Trotter has written about these 'unmarried widows' in '19th Century Emigration from Cornwall as Experienced by the Wives "Left Behind"' (PhD thesis, Exeter University, 2015).

9   *The Clarion* was a socialist weekly published in Manchester between 1891 and 1931. A number of clubs and associations (stretching from rambling and cycling groups to choral societies) were associated with the paper, and Gillian's ancestor, William Ranstead, sought to establish a *Clarion* colony when he moved out to New Zealand.

10 Bridget's experience appears to have been common. In the process of researching his book John came across a memorandum from the assistant colonial secretary of Tasmania to the colonial secretary in New Zealand in which the former is seeking reimbursement from the latter for the cost of getting the Kellys across to New Zealand. Another woman is named in the communication, which is itself 'part of a larger record'.

11 Rhonda Bartle suggests that between the Hangatāhua and Ōpunake, the South Road marked the border between the lowland bush and the flax: https://tinyurl.com/453nvypy

12 Maurice Shadbolt's story 'The People Before', on page 228 of which this quote can be found, is from his collection *Summer Fires and Winter Country* (Christchurch: Whitcombe & Tombs, 1963).

13 The *Fleming Pioneers Recalled* booklet is a classic of the family reunion genre. I recall attending the event but have no recollection of the congratulatory messages that Prime Minister Robert Muldoon, leader of the Opposition Bill Rowling and the leader of the Social Credit League Bruce Beetham apparently sent us all.

14 *Appendices to the Journals of the House of Representatives* (*AJHR*), 1883, A4, 5. The fracas also featured in an exchange between Hall and Governor Gordon on 24 October in which the former made the case for the invasion of Parihaka.

15 Alex Calder points out that an awful lot of New Zealand literature tells the story 'not [of] paradise made, but paradise lost'. This may be

so, but my sense is that because of the role they play in justifing our presence here most Pākehā family stories tend to the redemptive and the successful. These are generally good-news stories (albeit with zigs here and zags there). Alex Calder, *The Settler's Plot: How Stories Take Place in New Zealand* (Auckland: Auckland University Press, 2011), 135.

16   Trotter, '19th Century Emigration from Cornwall as Experienced by the Wives "Left Behind"', 260.

17   Colin Barr, 'The Irish College, Rome, and the Appointment of Irish Bishops to the United States, 1830–1851', in Daire Keogh and Albert McDonnell (eds), *The Irish College, Rome and its Worlds* (Dublin: Four Courts Press, 2008), 102–15.

18   In 1957, the penultimate year of his period as chairman, Taranaki beat Otago (11–9) to lift the Ranfurly Shield for the second time (the first followed a victory over Auckland in 1913). I have a photo of my grandfather standing outside the White Hart Hotel in New Plymouth congratulating Peter Burke, the Taranaki captain (and All Black). Tucked away in the Ngā Taonga Sound and Vision archives there is a 20-minute audio recording of that very welcome, roughly four minutes of which is taken up by Hughie talking flat out.

19   Te Rerenga Ora Iti, or Point Britomart, lies in the Waitematā Harbour in Tāmaki Makaurau Auckland. Prior to colonisation it had been a prominent headland. One of the first British military installations was established at Fort Britomart following the signing of Te Tiriti o Waitangi, but by the end of the 1880s the headland had been entirely quarried away. These days the area is best known as an urban transport hub.

20   When the AC was formally disbanded via the 1886 Defence Act, its policing and military functions were transferred to the New Zealand Police Force and the New Zealand Permanent Militia respectively.

21   I suspect she is right. The Naval and Military Settlers' and Volunteers' Land Act 1891 set out the arrangements for administering claims for land lodged by former military men. Grants were offered only to men who were fully retired from service. If McGrath transferred into the Police he was probably ineligible — as was my great-grandfather, who shifted directly from the AC into the Permanent Militia.

22   *New Zealand Parliamentary Debates (NZPD)*, 1879, vol. 34, 621; 797.

23   I have met three of Bryce's descendants. None of them knows either of the others, but each finds it hard work having him in their past.

24   Roth's words were recounted by Nathaniel Rich in the *New York Review of Books*, 28 June 2018, and I came across them in Keith Ovenden, *Bill and Shirley: A Memoir* (Auckland: Massey University Press, 2020), 161.

25 *Report to Waitangi Tribunal: Alienation of Land Within the Parihaka Block* (Wai 143, I17), 255. There were 57 sections in total in Block 12, so the Flemings were a major presence. I have a copy of a typed eight-page document (undated and unattributed) called simply 'Fleming History', and in it we can see the family's place in the social hierarchy being written into existence. The unknown author claims Michael Fleming as the first settler in the Pungarehu region; there is also speculation that perhaps the Cape Road branch of the Flemings was related to the 'rolled oats Flemings down south', which would, if true, have added a little lustre.

26 Kate Grenville, *A Room Made of Leaves* (Melbourne: Text, 2020), 18.

27 The quote is from Diana Bridge, *Deep Colour* (Dunedin: Otago University Press, 2023), 11.

28 Grenville, *A Room Made of Leaves*, 141.

29 Calder, *The Settler's Plot*, 87.

30 The phrase is from a parliamentary report tabled in 1885, in the midst of fears that had flared up amongst Taranaki settlers that Waikato Māori were on the verge of invading Taranaki. The document, 'Alleged Threatening Attitude of the Parihaka Natives Towards Europeans' (*AJHR*, 1885, G-4,1–9), contains a list of these concerns. They are odd and seemingly inconsequential. Mr Driller, for instance, had 'some little difficulty about pigs, when he says threats were used; but that is now all over, and he is the best of friends with the Natives.'

Chapter 3. Standing in the Shade

1 So says Haruki Murakami in *Killing Commendatore* (London: Harvill Secker, 2018), 57.

2 Keith Ovenden, *Bill and Shirley: A Memoir* (Auckland: Massey University Press, 2020), 166.

3 In 1886 the High Court in London ruled in favour of John Bryce, by now the MP for Wanganui, who had sued an Australian historian, George Rusden, for libel. The former native minister took exception to claims Rusden had made in his 1883 *History of New Zealand* that Bryce had 'gleefully' taken part in a massacre of Māori women and children near Whanganui in 1868. The court found that Rusden had got his facts wrong (there were no women at Handley's Woolshed) and he was required to pay significant damages to Bryce. John O'Leary assesses Rusden's motives and actions, as well as the boost the case gave to the imperial project — for Rusden had, in the view of the editorial writer at the *Auckland Star* on the day the decision was handed down, called into question the character not just of Bryce but also 'of the whole of our volunteers' (see John O'Leary,

'Too Good to be True? Race, Class, Massacre and the Bryce v Rusden Libel Case', *Journal of New Zealand Studies* 17 [2014]: 2–20). Vincent O'Malley sets out evidence provided during the libel trial by Ihaka Takarangi, one of the survivors of the attack at Handley's Woolshed, in *Voices from the New Zealand Wars He Reo nō ngā Pakanga o Aotearoa* (Wellington: Bridget Williams Books, 2021), 341–45.

4   Perpetual leases are, on the other hand, a thing in the South Island. In the early 1890s, the new Liberal government purchased a number of large estates and broke them up into smaller farms, offering them to farmers on 999-year leases at a fixed rent of 4 per cent of the original value of the land (Harry Evison, *Ngai Tahu Land Rights and the Crown Pastoral Lease Lands in the South Island of New Zealand*, 3rd edn [Christchurch: Ngāi Tahu Māori Trust Board, 1987], 65).

5   *Report to Waitangi Tribunal: Alienation of Land Within the Parihaka Block* (Wai 143, I17).

6   In Taranaki some 23,000 hectares of leasehold land are administered on behalf of owners by Parininihi Ki Waitōtara.

7   Waitangi Tribunal, *Taranaki Report: Kaupapa Tuatahi* (Wai 143) (Wellington: Waitangi Tribunal, 1996), 246.

8   *AJHR*, 1907, vol. 3, G–1c, 13–14.

9   Kavita Bedford, *Friends and Dark Shapes* (Melbourne: Text, 2021). My focus is on the untold stories of this country, but Gillian makes the very good point that '[m]any of the stories not told are of the way of life, the culture and traditions belonging with our own native lands, and what happened there, the hardships, terrors and traumas that took us from our homes' to this place.

10 Kiaran also remembers reading Belich's *The New Zealand Wars* and being struck by the conclusion that Tītokowaru had been 'forgotten as a child forgets a nightmare'. 'So very, very true for me,' he says.

11 It may also have helped assuage the dissonance — if such there was — of living on confiscated land that was smack bang in the middle of Ngāruahine's rohe. Certainly I can't recall, as someone raised in the Catholic faith, an awful lot of guidance coming from the top about how to resolve the sort of contradiction faced by Kiaran's ancestors. They will have had to figure that out themselves.

12 O'Malley's *Voices from the New Zealand Wars He Reo nō ngā Pakanga o Aotearoa* tells the story of the battle through the voices of those who were there.

13 Chapter 8 of O'Malley's *Voices from the New Zealand Wars He Reo nō ngā Pakanga o Aotearoa* covers the East Coast Wars.

14 John found this quote while researching the history of Bridget and

John Kelly. It is from Bryan Gilling, *Te Raupatu o Te Whakatōhea: The Confiscation of Whakatōhea Land 1865–1866* (Wellington: Waitangi Policy Unit, Department of Justice, 1994), 91. The estimates of the scale of the confiscation of land from Whakatōhea I use in this section are also from Gilling's work.

15 Nor did anyone else in his wife Trudi's immediate or wider family. That has since changed. John's original print run of 20 proved woefully inadequate, and at last count he had had to produce a further 80 copies of the book. There has been particular interest amongst the wider family in and around Ōpōtiki. In an email John noted that he had 'been down at their request to speak with about 25 of them, including descendants of the Māori part of the family (Bridget's eldest son, James, married a local Māori woman) who are Whakatōhea.' It was, he said, 'a most interesting day'.

16 In 1931 Ellen Foxon was the only Pākehā member of the institute, which she served in an advisory capacity. Later on, other Pākehā women also joined the organisation.

17 Ōtākou (1844), Canterbury (Kemp's) (1848), Port Cooper (1849), Port Levy (1849), Murihiku (1853), Akaroa (1856), North Canterbury (1857), Kaikōura (1859), Arahura (1860) and Rakiura (1864).

18 Evison, *Ngai Tahu Land Rights*, 23. Evison's book, a copy of which Marguerite sent me, contains a forensic analysis of the history and consequences of the Crown's actions in Te Wai Pounamu. Plenty of disturbing material in there, too, including threats made by Commissioner Henry Kemp that if Ngāi Tahu refused to sell they could look forward to being forced off the land by military force (p. 20), and the granting of 2560 acres to Mr Johnny Jones of Waikouaiti, which was more than had been provided for the 135 Māori living in the area (p. 23).

19 Both Evison's *Ngai Tahu Land Rights* and the Ngāi Tahu Claims Settlement Act 1998 refer to the nohoanga (seasonal occupation site) established at Te Ao Mārama (contemporary Ōmārama) by Te Maiharoa and around 100 of his followers in 1877. The settlement, which was roughly 8 acres in size, was destroyed by the AC in the winter of 1879.

20 Alex Calder, *The Settler's Plot: How Stories Take Place in New Zealand* (Auckland: Auckland University Press, 2011), 126.

21 My dad was a bit of an anomaly on the dishwashing front. Rather than sloping off for a snooze after a meal he would often volunteer to do the dishes. This trait (a legacy of having grown up in the Masterton Methodist Children's Home) endeared him to his mother-in-law, Milly, but made him an object of some suspicion to his father-in-law, Hugh. That he was a lousy card player did not help. What did help was having his arm mangled in the firing mechanism of a heavy artillery piece in his final stint of

compulsory military service. You can get away with drying any amount of dishes if you've done that.

22 Kate and Andrew (she 17 years younger than he) were married in the Ōkato Catholic church on 25 September 1898 by the French Marist Father Claudius Celestine Cognet. The wedding reception was held in the one-room schoolhouse in Pungarehu, which had previously seen service as the AC's blockhouse in which Te Whiti o Rongomai and Tohu Kākahi had been imprisoned for a month following the 1881 invasion. Andrew had been there for that, too, of course.

23 This phrase or an equivalent appears in each piece of legislation underpinning the settlements reached between the Crown and the eight Taranaki iwi (Ngāti Tama, Ngāti Ruanui, Ngaa Rauru Kiitahi, Ngāti Mutunga, Ngāruahine, Te Ātiawa, Taranaki and Ngāti Maru).

24 Waitangi Tribunal, *Taranaki Report: Kaupapa Tuatahi*, 238.

25 The quote is taken from: https://nzhistory.govt.nz/te-akomanga/contexts-activities/our-imperial-past-all-around-us

26 Joanna Kidman, Vincent O'Malley, Liana MacDonald, Tom Roa and Keziah Wallis, *Fragments from a Contested Past: Remembrance, Denial and New Zealand History* (Wellington: Bridget Williams Books, 2022), 93.

27 O'Malley, *Voices from the New Zealand Wars He Reo nō ngā Pakanga o Aotearoa*, 181.

28 Ibid., 175.

Chapter 4. How to Forget

1 Plenty of people have heard of Scott's 1975 *Ask that Mountain: The Story of Parihaka*, but *The Parihaka Story* — published in 1954 by Scott's own company, Southern Cross Books, and prompted by his reading of the Bryce v Rusden judgment — is less well known. Less well known still, I imagine, is that *The Parihaka Story* became the first New Zealand book published in Russian, when a Moscow publishing house ran off 15,000 copies in 'all caps Cyrillic' in 1957. This fascinating aside is from Mark Derby's tribute to Scott, 'The Weapon Beneath the Woodpile', in *Counterfutures: Left Thought and Practice Aotearoa* (2021), 71. Rachel Buchanan takes a look at that earlier publication in *The Parihaka Album*, assessing — not necessarily to Scott's advantage — the way in which Indigenous rights are linked to workers' rights (the focus of Scott's account of the 1951 waterfront dispute, *151 Days*). See Rachel Buchanan, *The Parihaka Album: Lest We Forget* (Wellington: Huia, 2009), 167–68.

2 Petition 2014/0037 of Waimarama Anderson and Leah Bell. The petition was signed by 12,000 people and presented at Parliament on 8 December

2015. The Māori Affairs select committee received 152 submissions on the petition, 138 of which opposed its aims. The committee delivered its final report on 19 December 2016. The entire record of those proceedings can be found here: https://tinyurl.com/c8e6myfa. For an analysis of the process, from start to finish, see chapter 4 of Joanna Kidman, Vincent O'Malley, Liana MacDonald, Tom Roa and Keziah Wallis, *Fragments from a Contested Past: Remembrance, Denial and New Zealand History* (Wellington: Bridget Williams Books, 2022).

3   A focus on what the British brought tends to overlook the things they took. Apropos, there is an episode of the excellent podcast *What the British Stole* that deals with taonga taken from Māori (www.abc.net.au/radionational/programs/stuff-the-british-stole/the-abductions/13572970).

4   On reflection, there may well be a fifth 'what about?', which is (e) What about the settlers? A particularly good example of this appeared in a review of Dick Scott's *The Parihaka Story* ran by the *Taranaki Herald* on 29 January 1955, in which Alexander Boyd Witten-Hannah 'wonders also, whether this will not be followed immediately by a book in reply with emphasis on the undoubted wrongs suffered by European settlers (for there was right and wrong on both sides)'. I came across this tawdry example of moral relativism in Virginia Winder's 2003 piece on Dick Scott, published on the Puke Ariki website (https://tinyurl.com/493tfca5).

5   Rachel Buchanan, *Te Motunui Epa* (Wellington: Bridget Williams Books, 2022), 119.

6   Paul Connerton, 'Seven Types of Forgetting', *Memory Studies* 1 (2008): 59–71.

7   Stuart Newall, after whom the Newall Road, which runs up towards the mountain from SH45, is named, was also an experienced road builder who had surveyed the area south of the Hangatāhua (Stony) River in 1880. Formerly a member of the Waikato Militia, he joined the AC in 1868, and before arriving in Taranaki in 1879 had taken part in the campaigns against both Tītokowaru and Te Kooti.

8   Buchanan, *The Parihaka Album*, 45.

9   Alex Calder, *The Settler's Plot: How Stories Take Place in New Zealand* (Auckland: Auckland University Press, 2011), 138.

10 Keith Ovenden, *Bill and Shirley: A Memoir* (Auckland: Massey University Press, 2020), 159.

11 This insight is from an episode of RNZ's *The Detail* that aired on 22 March 2022, in which Professor Macdonald discussed the new national histories curriculum. On the subject of which, Susan told me that when she first heard of the changes she 'didn't actually believe New Zealand history had not been part of the curriculum'. She was so surprised to hear that it

was not that she 'contacted the Department of Education, as I just didn't believe it'. She and quite a few others.

12   Elizabeth Strout, *My Name Is Lucy Barton* (New York: Vintage, 2016), 116.
13   Buchanan, *The Parihaka Album*.
14   Carolyn Morris, 'Not-Talking/Not-Knowing: Autoethnography and Settler Family Histories in Aotearoa New Zealand', *Genealogy* 6, no. 1 (2022): 10: https://doi.org/10.3390/genealogy6010010.
15   Edmund De Waal, *Letters to Camondo* (London: Penguin Random House, 2021), 17.
16   The reference to the apparatus is from Cormack McCarthy's *The Passenger* (London: Picador, 2022), 149.
17   Connerton, 'Seven Types of Forgetting', 59–71.
18   Ralph Hertwig and Dagmar Ellerbrock, 'Why People Choose Deliberate Ignorance in Times of Societal Transformation', *Cognition* 229 (2021): https://doi.org/10.1016/j.cognition.2022.105247
19   James Belich's *I Shall Not Die: Titokowaru's War, 1868–1869* (Wellington: Bridget Williams Books, 2010) is many readers' introduction to Tītokowaru. Vincent O'Malley sets out the background to the battle at Te Ngutu-o-te-Manu, and the wider campaign in south Taranaki, in chapter 9 of his *Voices from the New Zealand Wars He Reo nō ngā Pakanga o Aotearoa*.
20   The quote is taken from James Cowan, *The New Zealand Wars: A History of the Maori Campaigns and the Pioneering Period: Volume II: The Hauhau Wars: 1864–72* (Wellington: R. E. Owen, 1956), 206.
21   Vincent O'Malley, *Voices from the New Zealand Wars He Reo nō ngā Pakanga o Aotearoa* (Wellington: Bridget Williams Books, 2021), 336.
22   I would like to thank Kelvin Day for his guidance on and help with getting hold of the detail covered in this section. Kelvin's knowledge of the area around the coast is forensic, and he is very generous with it.
23   *AJHR*, 1871, D1, 5. The Hangatāhua, or Stoney — both names are used by the authorities — is at Ōkato, a little south of New Plymouth, while the Waingongoro is 5 kilometres north of Hāwera.
24   *AJHR*, 1872, G37, 3.
25   As part of this correspondence G. S. Cooper, an under-secretary to McLean, informs Parris that £400 has been authorised for the 'completion of the road from Stoney River southwards [to Warea], being the unfinished portion of the contract taken by the Ngamahanga' (*AJHR*, 1871, D1, 51). The government had also promised to return land confiscated from Ngā Māhanga a Tairi. But by 1879, when the Hon. Mr Sheehan, a member of the Cabinet, visited the area, he noted that mana whenua were expressing feelings of 'insecurity and distrust at the delay which has taken place in the completion of this transaction' (*AJHR*, 1879, C4, 2). Sheehan himself

accepted 'that our confiscation was never made complete according to Maori tikanga, by actual occupation'.

26 *AJHR*, 1871, D1, 78.

27 Wiremu Kīngi Moki Te Matakātea was a leading chief of the Ngāti Haumiti hapū of Taranaki iwi. He earned the name Te Matakātea — the clear eyed — for the accuracy of his shooting while resisting the siege of Te Namu pā, just north of Ōpunake, by Waikato Māori in 1833. An astute business person, by 1857 the income generated by his wheat and potato crops was supporting the construction of roading and educational infrastructure on his people's land. Three years later he was to play an important role in the first Taranaki War, when, as part of his resistance to land sales at Waitara, he led his people into battle against British troops and local volunteers at Waireka.

28 Ibid. The AC helped both build roads and protect them. At times the former was carried out with gusto: Inspector Scannell demurs in response to a request from Defence Minister Donald McLean for the names of those who 'display the most zeal and assiduity in carrying on roads and public works' in the Taupō region, finding it '[v]ery difficult to particularise any as shewing more zeal than the other where all are attentive' (*AJHR*, 1871, D1c, 8). As to the latter, at the AC's road camps in Taranaki, 'two guards, one of a sergeant and fifteen men, the other of a sergeant and six men, and a picquet of twenty constables and a sergeant, were detailed daily for duty. Special covering parties, of not less than a sergeant and twenty constables from each camp, were sent out daily for protection of the men working (who also took rifles with them)' (*AJHR*, 1880, H10, 23).

29 Surveying could be a fraught and troublesome business. In an 1875 review of the general state of surveys across the country, the chief surveyor in Taranaki, Mr Humphries, is reported as having found all 'the old work [undertaken in the 1860s] valueless for further use; many of the field-books are missing, and for miles together no original survey-marks can be found. He cannot tell what in it is right and what wrong' (*AJHR*, 1875, H1, 15).

30 *AJHR*, 1880, G-2, lvii–lvii.

31 Thomas Keneally, *The Great Shame* (London: Random House, 1998), 117.

32 *AJHR*, 1884, A5b, 4.

33 For there is 'the weighty consideration that the true solution of the trouble on the coast is, after all, occupation and settlement; and that, as on the Plains so even more certainly at the very doors of Parihaka, the establishment of English homesteads, and the fencing and cultivation of the land, will be the surest guarantee of peace' (*AJHR*, 1880, G2, lviii). And you're going to need that road to get the farmers onto the land, the stock to market and the milk to the factory.

34 *AJHR*, 1884, A5B, 3.

35 *AJHR*, 1880, F6, 3; see also *AJHR*, 1880, H10, 23.

36 *AJHR*, 1880, G2, lviii. The date of the original decision is taken from evidence given to the West Coast Commission at a meeting held in Waitara in March 1880 by Major Brown, the civil commissioner in Taranaki (*AJHR*, 1880, G2, 52). Brown also refers to 'negotiations entered into with Te Whiti and others respecting roads, telegraph lines, and the site of the proposed lighthouse at Cape Egmont' (*AJHR*, 1879, C4, 7), but I can't find any evidence of those discussions in the parliamentary record.

37 *AJHR*, 1879, C4, 10.

38 *AJHR*, 1881, H18, 2.

39 *AJHR*, 1881, H18, 2.

40 Rachel Buchanan, 'Orimupiko 22 and the Haze of History', *Journal of New Zealand Studies* 16 (2013): 71.

41 There are 14 others in Taranaki, the northernmost at Pukearuhe and the most southerly in Waverley. Information about those and other memorials to our wars are at: https://nzhistory.govt.nz/map/memorials-register-map. Details about the Katikara memorial can be found at: https://nzhistory.govt.nz/media/photo/katikara-memorial

42 The first chapter of Jock Phillips' *To The Memory: New Zealand's War Memorials* (Nelson: Potton & Burton, 2016) concerns the New Zealand Wars. One of its many fascinating details is that the very first memorial to the wars was not erected in this country at all; that distinction goes to the one constructed in 1850 at the Anglesea Barracks in Hobart, Australia, home for a time to the 99th Regiment, which fought in the Northern Wars. Phillips also points out that it is incorrect to assume (as Mark Twain did following his visit to Whanganui in 1895) that the 'brave men' who fell at Moutoa were all Englishmen: 15 of the names on that memorial are Māori from the lower Whanganui River, who died in the confrontation with Pai Mārire followers from Taranaki and the upper reaches of the river.

43 Kidman et al., *Fragments from a Contested Past*, 93. Next to the obelisk is a statue of man on a horse. We might naturally assume the man is Nixon, but that part of the edifice acknowledges the men from Ōtāhuhu who died during the First World War. The memorial to Nixon is one of just three that were erected by civilians to the dead of the New Zealand Wars (the other two are at Whanganui and New Plymouth); the remainder were the result of the efforts of imperial soldiers (Phillips, *To The Memory*, 20).

44 Scott Hamilton's *Ghost South Road* (Hamilton: Atuanui Press, 2018) tells that story.

45 The phrase is from someone who works close to the monument, and who was interviewed by Keziah Wallace (Kāi Tahu) and Liana MacDonald

(Ngāti Kuia, Rangitanē o Wairau, Ngāti Koata), for chapter 5 of Kidman et al., *Fragments from a Contested Past.*

46 Gillian goes on to say that Goldie 'was also the superintendent of city parks and wrote a chapter on the gardening year for Brett's Colonists' Guide and Cyclopaedia of Useful Knowledge'.

47 Avril Bell, 'Moving Roots: A "Small Story" of Settler History and Home Places', *Qualitative Inquiry* 23, no. 6 (2017): 452–57.

48 Ibid., 453.

Chapter 5. The Forgotten Country

1 Eddie's knowledge is voluminous and he has been exceptionally generous with it. In addition to the contents of various emails, he has sent me articles (some of which he has written, and one on Irish faction fighting authored by his son Matthew), newspaper clippings, photocopies of court records and land titles, genealogical detail and other miscellany. Virtually all of the detail in this section is from Eddie, and if I ever get to Ireland I will buy him a drink. Several, I would think.

2 One of the best treatments of this issue I've read is Dani's 'Harm Received, Harm Caused: A Scottish Gael's Journey to Becoming Pākehā', *Genealogy* 6 (2022): https://doi.org/10.3390/genealogy6040082

3 In the 1855 Griffith's, John Kennedy is recorded as leasing 58 statute acres and a house from William Anderson. (Griffith's valuation was carried out between 1848 and 1864 to determine someone's liability for payment of support for the poor and destitute within each Poor Law Union in Ireland.) On his death in 1862 this lease passed to Biddy Kennedy and thence, in 1864, to John's son Patrick (Hugh Gilhooly's brother-in-law). Twenty years later, in 1881, 28 acres transferred in the other direction, from Hugh to Patrick: Hugh was just five years from his own death from 'senile decay', and so was presumably unable to keep up with the work. At this point — and, ironically, in the very year Hugh's own son Andrew was involved in the invasion of Parihaka — the land formally leased to Mahoney, and subsequently split between the Kennedys and the Gilhoolys, was recombined. It was still leasehold land, though.

4 Eddie O'Dea tells me that the Kennedys are still in the parish and are 'now well respected'.

5 Sean Moraghan, 'The "Three Year Old" and "Four Year Old": Factions in County Limerick, *North Munster Antiquarian Journal* 59 (2019): 73–81.

6 Fox was at it again not long after this stint ended. In early October of 1879, Irish court records note that 'Michael Gillhooly, native of Ballingatly,

county Limerick, stands charged with having, on 8 September, 1879, at Ballinlough, in the barony of Small County, parish of Ballinlough, seriously assaulted Thomas Nihile with a loaded stick, fracturing his skull, thereby endangering his life'. The newspaper describes Fox thus: 'Cut mark on bridge of nose, wears all his beard; gray eyes, regular nose, fair complexion, oval face, stout make, 5 feet 8 inches high, about 30 years of age, brown hair; wore a dark tweed coat, trowsers, and vest. Is a farmer's son. This man is a returned convict, and was under Police supervision which ceased on 9th July last.' I'd have been inclined to stay out of his way.

7   Robert Macfarlane, *Mountains of the Mind: A History of a Fascination* (London: Granta, 2003), 6.

8   I had assumed that Andrew had been granted the family farms, but was wrong on two counts. For a start, as I've already noted, he had title to only one of them (Section 44 Block 12 of the Cape Survey District): his wife owned the second and the third was Māori land which he held under lease (albeit in perpetuity). Second, it appears that the one farm he did own was not granted to him on the basis of his military service. Under the provisions of the Naval and Military Settlers' and Volunteers' Land Act 1891, many former military men were entitled to grants of land in Taranaki, but Andrew's name is not on any of the lists of veterans whose claims for land were accepted, rejected or deemed ineligible (all of which are appended to the *Journals of the House of Representatives* [*AJHR*]). Instead, his certificate of title to Section 44 was granted under the 1892 Land Act, which dealt with the sale of Crown land (including confiscated land). I can't really figure it out and it probably doesn't much matter, because for both the Gilhoolys and mana whenua the end result is the same.

9   As it happens, it wasn't all that unusual for Irishmen to join either the Royal Irish Constabulary or the imperial regiments. In his *Police & Protest in England and Ireland 1780–1850* (Cambridge: Cambridge University Press, 1988), Stanley Palmer explains that in the 1870s over 75 per cent of the RIC's constables were Catholic (although Protestants made up 80 per cent of the officer class). Equivalent data aren't available for our own AC, but having waded through the archives, I have concluded that 89 of the 167 men who signed up in 1877, the year Andrew joined, had been born in Ireland (37 of them Catholics and the balance Protestants). On a related note, between 1792 and 1922, Irishmen comprised the single largest nationality within the entire British Army: see Peter Karsten, 'Irish Soldiers in the British Army, 1792–1922: Suborned or Subordinate?', *Journal of Social History* 17 (1983): 31–64. These 'green redcoats' were often 'a Catholic of low income, poorer than

those who took up arms against Britain from time to time, and poorer than those did not serve' (p. 37). Closer to home, John McLellan explains in 'Soldiers and Colonists: Imperial Soldiers as Settlers in Nineteenth-Century New Zealand' (Master's thesis, Victoria University, 2017) that the Irish comprised 20 per cent of those who served in British regiments between 1840 and 1870 and who chose to remain in New Zealand following discharge.

10 A lot has been written about the ways in which colonising powers impose laws from extant colonies in new territories. A good place to start is Lauren Benton, *Law and Colonial Cultures: Legal Regimes in World History, 1400–1900* (Cambridge: Cambridge University Press, 2002).

11 I cover the detail presented in this section in more detail in an article published in 2022, 'The Migratory Pathways of Labourers and Legislation: From Érin to Aotearoa', *Genealogy* 6: 83: https://doi.org/10.3390/genealogy6040083

12 *New Zealand Parliamentary Debates (NZPD)*, vol. E, 1864, 31. There is an enormous literature on the Royal Irish Constabulary. I would start with Robert Curtis, *The History of the Royal Irish Constabulary*, 2nd edn (Dublin: McGlashan & Gill, 1871) and Palmer, *Police & Protest in England and Ireland 1780–1850*.

13 *NZPD*, vol. 1(2), 1867, 481.

14 Ibid., 483.

15 Ibid., 482.

16 Ibid.

17 The best place to go for this is McLellan's 'Soldiers and Colonists'.

18 Waitangi Tribunal, *Taranaki Report: Kaupapa Tuatahi* (Wai 143) (Wellington: Waitangi Tribunal, 1996), 133.

19 *NZPD*, vol. D, 1863, 792.

20 Ibid., 860.

21 Waitangi Tribunal, *Taranaki Report: Kaupapa Tuatahi*, 133.

22 William Martin, 'Observations on the Proposal to Take Native Lands under an Act of the Assembly', *AJHR*, 1864, E-2, 7–8.

23 *NZPD*, vol. D, 1863, 870.

24 Alex Calder, *The Settler's Plot: How Stories Take Place in New Zealand* (Auckland: Auckland University Press, 2011), 110.

25 Tony Ballantyne, 'Mobility, Empire, Colonisation', *History Australia* 11 (2014): 22.

26 Linda Hardy's distinction between colonist as interloper and settler as natural occupant is in her essay 'Natural Occupancy', in Suvendrini Perera (ed.), *Asian and Pacific Inscriptions* (Bundoora, Vic: Meridian, 1995), 213–27.

27 I have Dani Pickering to thank for this insight. Of their own great-great-great-grandfather's 'assimilation into white New Zealand', Dani writes that '[a]lthough there is no obvious point at which one becomes the other within the narrative of the diaries, given the evidence it seems more likely to be Neil-as-Pākehā who had no observable qualms doing to Māori what had been done to him and his own people' (Pickering, 'Harm Received, Harm Caused', 12).

Chapter 6. Digging Up the Past

1 Stine Pilgaard, *The Land of Short Sentences* (New York: World Editions, 2022).
2 In 2019 the UK *Guardian* ran a series of reports on the Killing Times in Australia (www.theguardian.com/australia-news/2019/mar/04/the-killing-times-the-massacres-of-aboriginal-people-australia-must-confront). The extent to which the Native Police forced Indigenous Australians to fight and kill each other is also explored in Indigenous filmmaker Rachel Perkins' *The Australian Wars*, broadcast on Australia's SBS in 2022.
3 Rachel Buchanan, *The Parihaka Album: Lest We Forget* (Wellington: Huia, 2009), 71.
4 Dani Pickering is great on this. See 'Harm Received, Harm Caused: A Scottish Gael's Journey to Becoming Pākehā', *Genealogy* 6 (2022): https://doi.org/10.3390/genealogy6040082. I particularly like their no-nonsense view that 'it is misleading if not outright dishonest as a [Celtic] settler to evoke any historical trauma, any harm received [from English colonisers], without acknowledging historical privilege in the same breath, and the harm caused to attain it. In other words [in Aotearoa], it is simply not possible to be both coloniser and colonised at the same time . . . even with a family history that contains both.'
5 Melissa Lucashenko, 'Not Quite White in the Head', *Mānoa* 18, no. 2 (2019): 23–31.
6 One of the other murals is of Christ admonishing Thomas to believe. Thomas was the original empiricist, standing firm in his epistemological view that until he could 'see in his [Christ's] hands the mark of the nails, and place my finger into the mark of the nails, and place my hand into his side, I will never believe'. In the event he did what all good empiricists do when confronted with compelling material evidence: he changed his mind. The third mural was of the empty tomb, and was high on a wall on the western side of the foyer. Structural work was done on the church in the mid-1990s and it appears not to have been possible to keep the painting. The *Empty Tomb* had been the favourite

of Monsignor Carroll, the parish priest at St Joe's when I went there; the good Mons had died by the time the mural was removed, but would have been distressed at its loss. In 2001 Smither gave an interview to the Catholic publication *Tui Motu* (www.catholicparishnp.nz/assets/Michael-Smither-from-Tui-Motu-Issue-41-2001-May.pdf) in which he talks about those murals.

7   Adrienne Evans and Sarah Riley, 'The Righteous Outrage of Post-truth Anti-feminism: An Analysis of TubeCrush and Feminist Research In and Of Public Space', *European Journal of Cultural Studies* 25, no. 1 (2022): 25–42.

8   The adjectives are from a seven-and-a-half-hour exchange Mead and Baldwin had over two days in 1970, and which was subsequently published as *A Rap on Race* (New York: Corgi, 1971): https://archive.org/details/raponrace0000mead. The part about 'useful' guilt is on p. 67.

9   Le Guin's words are cited in an essay by Maria Popova at: www.themarginalian.org/2017/12/05/ursula-k-le-guin-no-time-to-spare-anger

10 Cormac McCarthy, *The Passenger* (New York: Knopf, 2022), 269.

11 www.themarginalian.org/2017/12/05/ursula-k-le-guin-no-time-to-spare-anger

12 Bill Pearson, 'Fretful Sleepers: A Sketch of New Zealand Behaviour and its Implications for the Artist', *Landfall* 6, no. 3 (1952): 202.

13 In 'The Unavailability of Nature: Anxieties of Place and Pākehā Identity in the Writings of Pip Adam, Robin Hyde, and Blanche Baughan' (Master's thesis, Massey University, 2020), Mel Ferguson explores how this anxiety manifests itself in our literature.

14 Avril Bell, 'Building Stamina, Fighting Fragility', *Ethnicities* 22, no. 5 (2022): 688.

15 Charles Mills, *The Racial Contract* (Ithaca, NY: Cornell University Press, 1997).

16 Benedict Anderson, *Imagined Communities* (London: Verso, 2006).

17 Which is what one of the characters does in Gillian's book *A Red Silk Sea* (Auckland: Penguin, 2005), much to the discomfort of the complacent locals.

18 Alfred Cox, *Recollections: Australia, England, Ireland, Scotland, New Zealand* (Christchurch: Whitcombe & Tombs, 1884), 148.

19 Dinah Hawken, *There Is No Harbour* (Wellington: Victoria University Press, 2019), 15.

20 Tim Shoebridge, *The Alienation of Maori Land in the Ohura South Block* (Wai 903 A67) (Wellington, Waitangi Tribunal, 2004), 13.

21 Rachel Buchanan, 'Orimupiko 22 and the Haze of History', *Journal of New Zealand Studies* 16 (2013): 67.

22 Charlotte Grimshaw, *The Mirror Book* (Auckland: Penguin Random House, 2021), 7.

23 Ibid., 20

24 Ibid., 23.

Chapter 7. Beneficiaries of Injustice

1   The title of this chapter is taken from Dinah Hawken's *There Is No Harbour* (Wellington: Victoria University Press, 2019), on p. 40 of which is written: 'I am the beneficiary of injustice.' As are many of us.

2   Charlotte Macdonald, 'From Woolwich to Wellington: From Settler Colony to Garrisoned Sovereignty', *New Zealand Journal of History* 53, no. 1 (2019): 50.

3   Keith Ovenden, *Bill and Shirley: A Memoir* (Auckland: Massey University Press, 2020), 33.

4   The 'bad history/good present' frame is from Avril Bell, 'Building Stamina, Fighting Fragility', *Ethnicities* 22, no. 5 (2022): 689.

5   From Owen Marshall, 'Family Ties', *Return to Harikoa Bay* (Auckland: Penguin Random House, 2022), 48.

6   There is a small universe of definitions to choose from. I've used the one by Linda Black and David Stone in 'Expanding the Definition of Privilege: The Concept of Social Privilege', *Journal of Multicultural Counselling and Development* 33, no. 4 (2011): 243–55.

7   The phrase is taken from Belinda Borell, Helen Moewaka Barnes and Tim McCreanor, 'Conceptualising Historical Privilege: The Flip Side of Historical Trauma, A Brief Examination', *AlterNative: An International Journal of Indigenous Peoples* 14, no. 1 (2018): 25–34.

8   Maria Tumarkin, *Traumascapes: The Power and Fate of Places Transformed by Tragedy* (Melbourne: Melbourne University Press, 2005), 12.

9   Robert Macfarlane, *Mountains of the Mind: A History of a Fascination* (London: Granta, 2003), 18.

10 Catherine Padmore, 'Telling Home Stories', *Life Writing* 6, no. 2 (2009): 270.

11 John Bluck, *Becoming Pākehā: A Journey Between Two Cultures* (Auckland: HarperCollins, 2022), 2.

12 Debbie Broughton, *The Ani Waaka Room* (Ōtaki: Te Tākapu, Te Wānanga Raukawa, 2022), 30.

13 Belinda Borell, Amanda Gregory, Tim McCreanor, Victoria Jensen and Helen Moewaka Barnes, '"It's hard at the top, but it's a lot easier than being at the bottom": The Role of Privilege in Understanding Disparities in Aotearoa/New Zealand', *Race/Ethnicity* 3 (2009): 35.

14 Broughton's poetry shreds Pākehā complacency, and Buchanan's tale of her tūpuna taonga is a thing of grace, beauty and many other things that are beyond my capacity to describe. You really should read both.

15 Avril Bell, 'Reverberating Historical Privilege of a "Middling" Sort of Settler Family', *Genealogy* 4, no. 46 (2020): doi: 10.3390/genealogy4020046

16 In this section I use the Reserve Bank of New Zealand's online calculator, which draws on historical quarterly consumer price index (CPI) data to estimate equivalent contemporary prices.

17 Waitangi Tribunal, Wai I17(g), 29.

18 Dick — or Ricardus, as he was known in Rome — is a favourite of mine. *The Forgotten Coast* was in part born out of a fascination I have had for my great-uncle for years. I grew up with scraps of stories: a brilliant young man who went to Rome, completed a Doctorate of Divinity, contracted TB and came home to die. And he *was* brilliant. He arrived at the Irish Pontifical College in 1930 and within 18 months had completed three degrees: a Baccalaureates, his Licentiate and the doctorate. The doctoral programme alone was supposed to take four years. He was so young when he finished his academic work that he had to seek a papal dispensation to be ordained a priest: in fact, he had to wait a year before he was old enough even to apply for the dispensation. And he was a consumptive, as they would have said then. He contracted TB while preparing for his doctoral examination, was shipped home in 1932 and spent the next 22 years slowly dying.

19 Michael Fleming, Kate Gilhooly's older brother, was a foundation member of the first of these companies and its chairman of directors for 34 years. The Fleming history booklet mentions that he was also 'a Commissioner into Parihaka', but I haven't been able to find his name in the parliamentary record in this capacity. It also says he once lost £10,000 when the share price of a local fertiliser company crashed.

20 Borell, Moewaka Barnes and McCreanor, 'Conceptualising Historical Privilege', 28.

21 Buchanan, 'Orimupiko 22 and the Haze of History', 71.

22 Wai 143 I17, 188.

Chapter 8. Doing Stuff

1 Diana Bridge uses the Sebald quote as an epigraph in her *Deep Colour* (Dunedin: Otago University Press, 2023).

2 Alice Procter, *The Whole Picture: The Colonial Story of the Art in Our Museums & Why We Need to Talk About It* (London: Cassell, 2020), 10–11.

3 Rebecca Solnit, *Orwell's Roses* (London: Granta, 2021), 104.

4 The line is paraphrased by LCD Soundsystem's thumpingly good 'Losing My Edge'. Play often and loud.

5 The 2013 report of the Independent Police Conduct Authority (IPCA) into

what was known as Operation Eight presents one view of what occurred in Te Urewera in 2007. The IPCA concluded that the decision of the police commissioner to 'terminate' the activities of 'a group of people who appeared to be involved in military style training camps using firearms and other weapons in remote forest areas within the Urewera Ranges was reasonable and justified in the circumstances' (*Operation Eight: The Report of the Independent Police Complaints Authority* [Wellington: IPCA, 2013], 5). But it also found that elements of the operation 'were contrary to law and unreasonable', including the setting up of roadblocks at Ruatoki and Tāneatua and the personal searches and detention of a number of people (p. 7). Others, of course, see the affair very differently. In the event, no prosecutions were sought under the Terrorism Suppression Act 2002, although charges were laid under the Arms Act 1983 and the Crimes Act 1961. In late 2011 the Supreme Court dismissed charges against 13 people. In April 2013 it upheld convictions (and sentencing) against four others. Two people were sentenced to nine months' home detention and two others to two and a half years in prison.

6   In 2014, two years after Joe was invited to Maungapōhatu, Tūhoe settled its Treaty claim with the Crown. As part of the settlement the Crown apologised for its historic misdeeds, including land confiscations; indiscriminate killings, including of women and children; and scorched-earth warfare. Ngāi Tūhoe's website carries Minister Chris Finlayson's address on the day the claim was settled. Reading it (www.ngaituhoe. iwi.nz/news-feed/id/444), it's easy to see why Joe considered his visit to Maungapōhatu a significant moment.

7   Richard Hill, *The Colonial Frontier Tamed: New Zealand Policing in Transition: 1867–1886*, the second volume of Hill's monumental *The History of Policing in New Zealand* (Wellington: Department of Internal Affairs, 1989), 1.

8   The contemporary effort is being led by Rev. Tom Williams, whose own grandmother was a friend of Marguerite's grandmother, and whose grandfather, Tom, sheared the sheep on the Foxons' Winchester farm.

9   This translation is from John Dunn's beautiful meditation on democracy, *Setting the People Free: The Story of Democracy* (London: Atlantic Books, 2005), 27. Dunn explains that the oration was written by the historian Thucydides, who assures us that what he has Pericles say is what Pericles said.

10 'Every inquiry replaces what is addressed': Cormac McCarthy, *The Passenger* (New York: Knopf, 2022), 128.

11 Owen Marshall, *Return to Harikoa Bay* (Auckland: Penguin Random House, 2022), 130.

Chapter 9. Becoming

1   The term is from Peter Wells and Rex Pilgrim (eds), *Best Mates: Gay Writing in Aotearoa New Zealand* (Auckland: Penguin, 1997), but I came across it in Paul Diamond, *Downfall: The Destruction of Charles Mackay* (Auckland: Massey University Press, 2022), 8.

2   Rachel Buchanan, *Te Motunui Epa* (Wellington: Bridget Williams Books, 2022), 23.

3   Buchanan tells this story in 'There's a Buried Forest on My Land', in Jolisa Gracewood and Susanna Andrews (eds), *Tell You What: Great New Zealand Nonfiction 2015* (Auckland: Auckland University Press, 2015), 124–31. She has identified at least 21 pieces of legislation that apply to the land.

4   Ibid., 126.

5   The irony is that Yeats's fearful poem was written in the shattered aftermath of the First World War, itself the genesis of the narrative that New Zealand came of age as a nation on the shores of Anzac Cove, a foundation story that has long overshadowed the wars that took place on our own soil.

6   Joan Didion, *Slouching Towards Bethlehem* (New York: Farrar, Strauss & Giroux, 2008).

7   Lucy Mackintosh, *Shifting Grounds: Deep Histories of Tāmaki Makaurau Auckland* (Wellington: Bridget Williams Books, 2021), 221.

8   Alex Calder, *The Settler's Plot: How Stories Take Place in New Zealand* (Auckland: Auckland University Press, 2011), 112.

9   Avril Bell, 'Decolonizing Conviviality and "Becoming Ordinary": Crosscultural Face-to-Face Encounters in Aotearoa New Zealand', *Ethnic and Racial Studies* 39, no. 7 (2016): 1175.

10 From Joshua Cohen, *The Netanyahus* (New York: New York Review Books, 2021), 31.

11 The quote is from a piece published on *The Spinoff* website on 7 March 2020 called 'Where to next? Decolonisation and the stories in the land'. Jackson's chapter 'Where to Next? Decolonisation and the Stories in the Land', builds on this thesis and is in Bianca Elkington et al., *Imagining Decolonisation* (Wellington: Bridget Williams Books, 2020).

12 Fred Vargas, *The Three Evangelists* (London: Vintage, 1995), 147.

13 Bell, 'Decolonizing Conviviality and "Becoming Ordinary"', 1174.

14 Writing about Kurt Vonnegut's *Slaughterhouse-Five* in *The Atlantic* in March 2019, James Parker refers to a sermon Paul Tillich once gave in which the theologian reflected that, following his unseating by celestial forces on the road to Damascus, the apostle Paul 'dwelt with the pieces' of his shattered psyche rather than trying to put them back together again.

15 Ursula Le Guin, 'Introduction to Rocannon's World', in Brian Attebery (ed.), *Ursula K. Le Guin: Hainish Novels & Stories*, vol. 1 (New York: The Library of America, 2017), 761.

16 Ralph Hertwig and Dagmar Ellerbrock, 'Why People Choose Deliberate Ignorance in Times of Societal Transformation', *Cognition* 229 (2021): 6: https://doi.org/10.1016/j.cognition.2022.105247

17 Robert Macfarlane, *Mountains of the Mind: A History of a Fascination* (London: Granta, 2003), 178.

18 *Appendices to the Journals of the House of Representatives (AJHR)*, 1880, G2, lxiii.

19 *AJHR*, 1871, D1, 75.

20 Macfarlane, *Mountains of the Mind*, 191.

Acknowledgements

There's a thing that sometimes happens when people talk with me about *The Forgotten Coast*. They'll say how they enjoyed this bit but were less taken by that part. I'll thank them for having read the book, there will be a small pause, as if they are weighing up how or whether to shift gears — and then they will quietly start unrolling their own small story.

That is pretty much how this book has come to be; all it has required is me sitting down and listening to, and then reflecting on, the things that people know, or don't know, about where they come from. It has been the most remarkable privilege to be afforded glimpses into what Owen Marshall calls in his short story 'The Drummer and the Stoat Killer' (*Return to Harikoa Bay*, 2022) the 'small cosmos' of people's worlds.

Some of this book's content comes from the extensive email correspondence I received following publication of *The Conversation* article and *The Forgotten Coast* in 2021. Most of it, however, is drawn from a series of surveys and interviews completed in late 2022 and early 2023, and from the lengthy correspondence surrounding those conversations. My thanks go to all of those who took the time to talk with me, either virtually or in person.

In particular, I want to acknowledge those who have let me use their names. The standard practice when inviting people to participate in a project like this is to treat their contributions anonymously. There are good reasons for doing this, most of which have to do with keeping people safe. But some of those I spoke with wanted to stand by what they had to say. Good for them — it's a courageous thing to do.

And so my especial thanks go to Aidan Bright, Marguerite Foxon, John Grant, Joe Green, Susan Grimsdell, Jane Julian, Tim Julian, Kiaran King, David McKay, Dorothy McKay, Win (Johnson) McMinn, Gillian Ranstead, Justine Skilling and Susan Smith (RNDM). Thank you, too, to those who completed lengthy surveys but did so on the basis of anonymity: your words are every bit as significant as those of others. And to Barbara Henley (RNDM), thank you for helping this book come to completion.

John Grant gets a special mention for having allowed me to borrow liberally from his history of John and Bridget Kelly. So, too, do Kelvin Day and Eddie O'Dea, the former for his advice and guidance on all matters concerning the South Road (and Taranaki in general) and the latter for introducing me to the Irish Gilhoolys.

Unless you are a complete tosser, one of the things you learn to do as an academic is to let other people read your work before it goes anywhere near a wider audience. These people save you from making embarrassing mistakes (such as omitting the letter 'l' from the word public, which a spell checker will not pick up), or worse. They also ask probing questions, metaphorically walking around your work and wondering if perhaps this or that part might need a bit of a rethink.

My saviours in this case include Janine Hayward, whose sense of humour is matched by her acumen, eye for detail and generosity with all things; and Ella Kahu, Carolyn Morris, April Bennett, Matt Wynyard and Colin Bjork, who are good colleagues and better friends. Carolyn, who is a woman of many talents, also created the art which graces the cover of this book — an embroidered curtain which generally hangs in her dining room window and which photographer Dave Wiltshire helped convert from one thing to another. Taranaki maunga dominates Carolyn's *The Agricultural Campaign*, but look carefully and you will also see the bushline, ploughed fields and broken fences. Echoes of times past which resonate now. I thought it would make a wonderful cover and I am so grateful that Carolyn agreed.

Once again I find myself indebted — in the best possible way — to Nicola Legat and her team at Massey University Press. Nicola saw something in *The Forgotten Coast* and has also backed this book. She has also given me — twice now! — the glorious gift of being able to step beyond the confines of academic writing. Nicola: I can't tell you how good for my soul that is. And to everyone else at MUP, including Emily Goldthorpe: thank you for the gorgeous books you bring into our world.

A special word of thanks to Jane Parkin, who was an absolute joy to work with. Jane's graceful, light touch and eye for balance and harmony made this a far better book than it was when she received the manuscript, and I think it would be a very good thing indeed if she could edit everything I write — academic or otherwise — from here on out.

To Trudie Cain and Ella Kahu: you fullaesses are the best people I have ever worked with, and neither this book nor *The Forgotten Coast* would have been written had we not teamed up on Tū. Thank you for all you have taught me.

I want to end by acknowledging my partner, Ema, who has lived a life far from her own mountains and rivers. Exiled from her *terroir*, she has, nonetheless, the grace and decency to read my attempts to get to grips with my own. Toujours, ma belle.

About the Author

Richard Shaw is a professor of politics at Massey University's College of Humanities and Social Sciences. He is a regular commentator on political issues and the author of a number of academic publications about government, parliament and politics in Aotearoa New Zealand. His heart increasingly lies in the historical and emotional territories explored both in this and his 2021 book, *The Forgotten Coast* (Massey University Press).

MASSEY
UNIVERSITY
PRESS

First published in 2024 by Massey University Press
Private Bag 102904, North Shore Mail Centre
Auckland 0745, New Zealand
www.masseypress.ac.nz

Design by Carolyn Lewis
Cover artwork: Carolyn Morris, *The Agricultural Campaign*, 2002, embroidered
curtain, 1540 × 1770 mm

Extracts published with permission: 'The re-Taranaki-fication of Te Aro Pā'
(pages 5 and 147) and 'But for Ngā Rangahautira and Māori Lecturers'
(page 143), by Debbie Broughton, originally published in *The Ani Waaka
Room* (Ōtaki: Te Tākapu, Te Wānanga Raukawa, 2022).

A catalogue record for this book is available from the National Library
of New Zealand

Printed and bound in China by Everbest Printing Investment

ISBN: 978-1-99-101668-3
eISBN: 978-1-99-101669-0

The publisher gratefully acknowledges the assistance of Creative New Zealand.

creative nz
ARTS COUNCIL OF NEW ZEALAND TOI AOTEAROA